Philadelphia

A Pictorial Celebration

Alice L. George, Ph.D.

Photography by Elan Penn

Sterling Publishing Co., Inc.
New York

Design by Michel Opatowski
Edited by J. E. Sigler
Layout by Gala Pre Press Ltd.

Penn Publishing gratefully acknowledges the following institutions
and individuals for allowing photographs from their collections to be
reproduced in this book:

African-American Museum in Philadelphia 141
Congregation Mikveh Israel 34
Greg Fiume/New Sport/Corbis 132–133
Kimmel Center for the Performing Arts
Jeff Goldberg/Esto 152
Roman Violy 153
Lee Snider/Photo Images/Corbis 58
Library of Congress 6–16

Pennsylvania Academy of Fine Arts
Rick Echelmeyer 147 top
Tom Crane 147 bottom
Philadelphia Academy of of Music, photos by
Nick Kelsh 148–149
Philadelphia Museum of Art 151
Union League 94–95

Library of Congress Cataloging-in-Publication Data

George, Alice L., 1952–
Philadelphia : a pictorial celebration / by Alice L. George ; photography by Elan Penn.
    p.   cm.
Includes index.
ISBN-13 : 978-1-4027-2384-1
ISBN-10: 1-4027-2384-9
    1.Philadelphia (Pa.)—Pictorial works. 2. Philadelphia (Pa.)—History. 3.
    Philadelphia (Pa.)—Description and travel. I. Penn, Elan, ill. II. Title.

F158.37. G46 2006
974-8'1100222-dc22

20050563344

2 4 6 8 10 9 7 5 3 1

Published by Sterling Publishing Co., Inc.
387 Park Avenue South, New York, NY 10016
© 2006 by Penn Publishing Ltd.
Distributed in Canada by Sterling Publishing
c/o Canadian Manda Group, 165 Dufferin Street
Toronto, Ontario, Canada M6K 3H6
Distributed in the United Kingdom by GMC Distribution Services
Castle Place, 166 High Street, Lewes, East Sussex, England BN7 1XU
Distributed in Australia by Capricorn Link (Australia) Pty. Ltd.
P.O. Box 704, Windsor, NSW 2756, Australia

Sterling ISBN-13: 978-1-4027-2384-1
ISBN-10: 1-4027-2384-9

For information about custom editions, special sales, premium and
corporate purchases, please contact Sterling Special Sales
Department at 800-805-5489 or specialsales@sterlingpub.com.

Opposite: The Schuylkill River and Philadelphia skyline.

Contents

Philadelphia: Birthplace of American Liberty

When Americans think of Philadelphia today, many of them probably still conjure up images of cobblestone streets and men in white wigs. Certainly, the city's moment in the sun as both national and state capital—not to mention as the nucleus of precedent-setting activity for the whole world—continues to influence and enrich its streets and its citizens today. Philadelphia's history did not end with the signing of the Constitution, however. Indeed, the city William Penn planned between the Delaware and Schuylkill Rivers is ever balancing itself between two shores: the glorious bank of American revolution, independence, and freedom and the cutting edge of her nation's bright and promising future.

At the beginning of the twenty-first century, Philadelphia was the nation's fifth-largest metropolitan area. Accordingly, visitors to the area quickly observe that the city is not merely a shrine celebrating the big events of the past, but a dynamic metropolis accustomed to using its inborn ingenuity to reinvent its surroundings to meet current needs. At the same time, Philadelphians do harbor a profound respect for their history, and this has led to preservation. More recently, their equally strong appreciation of art and culture has also brought many masterpieces to the Delaware Valley. The result is a treasure trove of precious sites and moving reminders capable of cultivating in any American heart a deep pride in this nation's heritage.

Unfortunately, the area's first inhabitants, the Lenni Lenape, or Delaware Indians, left few traces of their inhabitancy behind. However, the Europeans who followed them built a visible record of the city's development. The first Europeans to visit the area were traders who merely met the Indians, traded goods with them, and left. It didn't take long for those passers-through to carry word back to the Old World of the area's rich resources and desirability for settlement. Soon, settlers arrived in abundance, shaping the city first into the largest and most vibrant city of the British colonies, then into the temporary capital of the new American republic, then into a thriving and prosperous center of manufacturing and culture . . . and that is only the beginning of the story of Philadelphia.

Philadelphia.

Philadelphie.

Houses of Worship and War: Remnants of Early American Life

The first non-natives to build a community in what is now Philadelphia were the Scandinavian settlers who built Gloria Dei Church. Fifty Scandinavian farmers who had settled between the Delaware and Schuylkill Rivers built the church in 1700 to house the

View of Philadelphia by Balthasar F. Leizelt, 1770s.

The city of Philadelphia, 1875.

Lutheran congregation they had formed fifty years before. Gloria Dei, now Episcopalian, is the oldest standing church in Philadelphia and one of the earliest remaining signs of European habitation here.

The founding of Christ Church in 1695 reflected significant English migration into the city. In 1681, King Charles II chose William Penn as the colony's proprietor, and Penn's first decision in that position drew settlers by the shipful. Considering the colony a "holy experiment," he guaranteed Pennsylvanians freedom from the divisive religious persecution faced by Quakers, Puritans, and other dissenters from the Church of England. At first, a simple wooden church was constructed for the colony's new Anglican community; by 1744 it had been replaced by the grand architectural showcase that is Christ Church today.

Penn planned for civil freedom as well as religious, and made provisions for a representative government and a generally peaceful environment. Evidence that his colony was indeed uniquely democratic for the times is easily found at the Mikveh Israel Cemetery, where many

historic grave markers testify to the presence of a thriving Jewish community within the colony by the time of its official founding in 1740. Additionally, the Great Quaker Meeting House near Christ Church and the Old Pine Street Church, the oldest Presbyterian church in Philadelphia, received two more persecuted congregations from abroad into Penn's "City of Brotherly Love."

While in the colony on his first two-year visit from 1682 to 1684, Penn developed good relations with the Lenni Lenape and bought from them the land that now makes up Philadelphia, Bucks, and Chester Counties. Because he expected no danger from the neighboring Indians (who already had begun moving westward), Penn refused to build his city like a fortress. On the contrary, in October 1682, he ordered architect Sir Thomas Holme to plan a sprawling, expansive town with the Delaware River as its eastern boundary and the Schuylkill River as its western edge. The following year, Holme's *Portraiture of the City of Philadelphia* was published in London, picturing evenly spaced, wide streets set out in a rectangular

MVS227. PAINTING BY DUNSMORE   WASHINGTON AND LAFAYETTE AT VALLEY FORGE   COPYR

Washington and Lafayette at Valley Forge by John W. Dunsmore, circa 1907.

grid—a pattern still evident in Center City Philadelphia.

However, Penn's vision of a town that stretched from river to river would not become reality as quickly as he dreamed. Initial growth occurred primarily on the city's eastern side, in the few blocks closest to the Delaware River. As residents crowded together in tight quarters, many tiny streets had to be improvised within Holme's grand plan. Development of Elfreth's Alley, now the oldest continuously occupied residential street in the nation, reflects this common pattern in the new city. Head House Square, located in the center of Second Street, was also a result of such overcrowding. Originally known as "New Market," it was created in 1745 to relieve some of the congestion at the city's first market on High Street. Eventually, Penn's dream of an open, spacious town would come true, but not until the nineteenth century, when Philadelphians finally began building homes near the shores of the Schuylkill River.

Other telltale signs of a booming settlement began popping up around Philadelphia early on. In 1741, the city opened its most revered landmark, the State House, and twelve years later the beloved Liberty Bell tooks its place in the building's tower. Over time, the State House's central role in the cause for independence would change its name in the popular mind—though not officially—to Independence Hall. Right on the heels of this first government building came the town's first hospital: Pennsylvania Hospital, now the oldest hospital in the United States, opened in 1752 by Benjamin Franklin, Dr. Thomas Bond, and others.

Naturally, "the quintessential Philadelphian," as he is called, is honored throughout the city. In his many contributions to his adopted hometown and in its tributes to him, Benjamin Franklin is still very much alive here. Franklin Court marks the site where he settled shortly after arriving in the city in 1723, and the

General George Washington in prayer at Valley Forge.

Benjamin Franklin National Memorial honors him for his many scientific, academic, diplomatic, and political achievements.

Franklin's name is without a doubt the biggest name ever to become attached to the city, but many other great names left their mark on Philadelphia as well, especially during the turbulent times in which Franklin lived. On the eve of the Revolutionary War, Thomas Jefferson sat writing the Declaration of Independence at the Graff House on Seventh and Market Streets. Betsy Ross, according to legend, sat sewing the first American flag at her home on Arch Street. When war finally broke out, Philadelphians saw history being made all around them: At the Brandywine Battlefield State Park, within earshot

of Philadelphia, General George Washington's forces were defeated on September 11, 1777. Cliveden, a Germantown mansion, became the unlikely site of another battle when British troops under attack were forced to take refuge there. Valley Forge National Historic Park marks the area where General Washington and his men endured that infamous winter after losing the Battle of Germantown. After the British captured Philadelphia in September 1777, soldiers at Old Ford Mifflin on the Delaware River tried to stop enemy ships from re-supplying troops in the city. After British forces evacuated the city in June 1778, the city began the process of reconstruction. However, it was not until the fighting finally ended once and for all in October 1781 that citizens could really rejoice—for now they were free! In 1787, the joy in Philadelphia was multiplied when the town won the privilege of welcoming George Washington and the Constitutional Conventions at Independence Hall. When the Constitution won approval, some Philadelphians hoped that the national government would leave its current home in New York to settle in the Quaker City. Indeed, the government would leave its home in New York to settle in Philadelphia—but only temporarily, while lawmakers waited for planners to develop a new capital on the Potomac: Washington, D.C.

After the Capital: Nineteenth-Century Landmarks

In June 1800, the federal government moved to Washington, D.C., as it had planned. The year before, Lancaster had replaced Philadelphia as capital of Pennyslvania, too. Suddenly, Philadelphians felt like they had been thrust from center-stage off the stage entirely, and the city faced an uncertain destiny. Since their future was clearly not going to be in government, citizens would have to make like ol' Ben and show ingenuity. By combining commerce, industry, and culture, they succeeded at bringing

Philadelphia back to prosperity by the end of the century.

In the beginning, though, the city didn't have much going for it except for its glorious history and its rich culture. As work began to transform the city into an industrial center, Philadelphia unexpectedly found itself becoming a new magnet to tourists. While trying to solve normal city problems, it just happened to do such a good job that people flocked to see the results.

The Fairmount Waterworks, for example, started out as nothing more than a practical effort to provide clean water for the city. But because the designers achieved ingenious feats of engineering and found creative ways to make the site both functional and lovely, by 1822 it was a huge tourist attraction. Similarly, Eastern State Penitentiary, opened in 1829, became another unlikely magnet for tourists. There, the city had inadvertently built an architectural curiosity and established in it a prison system modeled on the latest correctional theories—interesting stuff for the nineteenth-century traveler.

The city soon learned the value of those accidental attractions and began making a deliberate effort to draw visitors to town. In 1874, it opened its first intentional hot spot, the Philadelphia Zoo, still the oldest zoo in the nation. Two years later, another successful attraction brought visitors flooding into the city: the Centennial Exposition in Fairmount Park. Memorial Hall, the only building left standing from that event, was transformed into the Philadelphia Museum of Art, and is now home to the Please Touch Museum.

Philadelphia achieved its goal of becoming a national industrial leader, making everything from textiles to umbrellas to ten-gallon hats. In 1854, the city and county of Philadelphia consolidated, bringing into the city the busy manufacturing areas—Manayunk, Bridesburg, Southwark, and Kensington—that had once been outside of town. With this single action, the city grew from four square miles to 130 square miles, and its primary source of income shifted from shipbuilding and port-based businesses to industry and manufacturing.

As technological advancement propelled the city forward—except for City Hall, of course, whose construction it dragged out mercilessly— the telltale signs of industrialization began springing up along the railroad tracks leading out of town. As the manufacturing city got blacker and uglier, those who could afford it headed out of the city to found suburbs in the area along the Main Line. Many of them built fine estates in Bucks, Chester, and Montgomery Counties, where they lived luxurious country lives between rail commutes into the city.

As the process of suburbanization suggests, however, the nineteenth century was not all

Benjamin Franklin by N. Currier, 1847.

success and progress. When members of the middle class began to follow the wealthy out of downtown, they left behind a city of blue-collar workers. The conditions in most factories were notoriously poor, and the pollution they created was obviously anything but healthful to nearby residents. In the century's first half, mob violence was not uncommon. While Catholics later were able to build the beautiful Cathedral of Saints Peter and Paul, many poor Catholic immigrants faced ugly xenophobic violence before 1850. Fierce opposition to abolitionists also was a problem, but when the Civil War began, the city stood behind the Union through organizations such as the new Union League. And as the city was inundated with poverty-stricken new immigrants, Eastern State Penitentiary grew overcrowded as well—and *not* with tourists.

Nevertheless, as some citizens persecuted, hated, and killed, others fought for equality, love,

Pre-Revolutionary taverns and inns in Philadelphia, circa 1908.

and peace. As the statue *Religious Liberty* which still stands at the National Museum of American Jewish History testifies to this day, even nineteenth-century Philadelphia wasn't as far from William Penn's original dream of a "City of Brotherly Love" as it could have been.

E Pluribus Unum: Greater Philadelphia Today

What Philadelphia had going for it at the turn of the twentieth century was its awareness that its downtown core was in decline. The longer the city waited to turn things around, however, the steeper the descent grew. Just between 1900 and 1915, a flood of immigration increased the population downtown by almost one-third. Shabby tenements sprang up all over town, and the city limits all but burst with unskilled workers and unemployed—and that was *before* the Great Depression.

The city chose to counter the problem in a few different ways: One was to fund construction projects that would improve the city's means of public transportation, thus creating work for some residents while making it easier for others to find work outside their neighborhoods. Another ingenious idea was to begin beautifying the city itself to make it a more pleasant place to live and to tempt wealthy suburbanites to at least come spend some of their money downtown. Finally, higher emphasis was placed on educational opportunities within the city, which quite simply benefited everybody. Together, these three improvement programs—transportation, recreation, and education—marked the last eighty years of the twentieth century as well as the beginning of the twenty-first.

The improvements began in the 1920s with the construction of two major thoroughfares. The Benjamin Franklin Parkway, a grand boulevard leading to many of the city's finest cultural

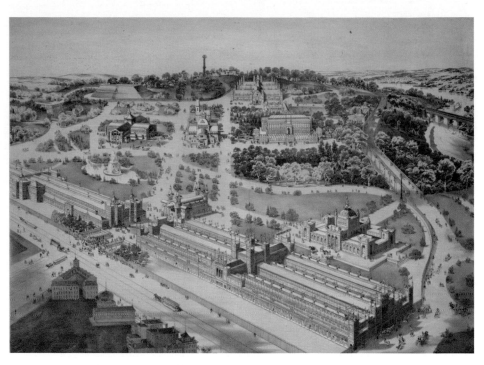

Buildings and grounds of International Exhibition, Fairmont Park, by August L. Weise, circa 1876.

institutions, both eased travel across the city and provided an impetus for beautification of the surrounding area. Similarly, the Benjamin Franklin Bridge, which was the world's longest suspension bridge at the time of its completion, served two inseparable purposes, one practical and one uplifting: it made the commute across the Delaware River between Philadelphia and New Jersey much easier, and it added considerable beauty to the city's skyline.

In the 1930s, the city moved on to build the nation's largest train station, Thirtieth Street Station. A living monument to the railroad age, the elegant station is still the country's second-most active. The Reading Terminal Headhouse and Market was the target of a different approach. Built in 1893, the station was made obsolete in 1984 and so converted into a glorious entrance to the Philadelphia Convention Center. Now the beloved structure attracts more than 80,000 shoppers and hungry diners per week.

Although not a project undertaken by the city, the construction of Liberty Place in the late 1980s changed the city's skyline and its visual image dramatically. The two towers made history when they became the first city skyscrapers to exceed the height of the William Penn statue at the top of City Hall, a mark not exceeded by unwritten rule for almost a century. Now, the two glass towers are the most recognizable features in the city's skyline.

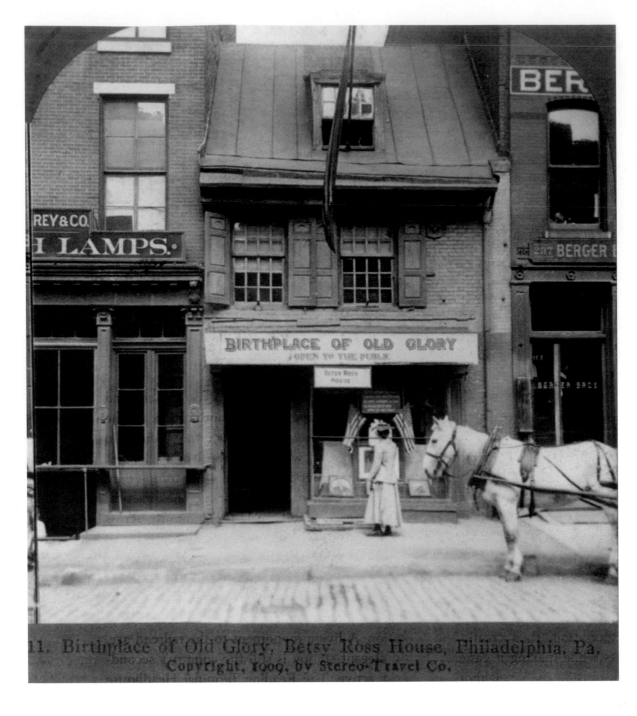

11. Birthplace of Old Glory, Betsy Ross House, Philadelphia, Pa.
Copyright, 1909, by Stereo-Travel Co.

Birthplace of Old Glory, Betsy Ross House, circa 1903.

Throughout the city, and especially along the Benjamin Franklin Parkway, Philadelphia was made to bloom and blossom in the twentieth century. Rittenhouse Square and Logan Circle, both among William Penn's original green spaces in his plan for Philadelphia, have become magnets for Philadelphians seeking quiet, sunny relaxation. And whether it's Robert Indiana's twenty-foot-high "LOVE" sculpture at John F. Kennedy Plaza, Claes Oldenburg's *Clothespin* sculpture across the street from City Hall, *The Cowboy* by Frederic Remington, or any of the seventeen sculptures on display at the E. P. Samuel Memorial Sculpture Garden, a master-

piece of outdoor art seems to be lurking around every corner in Philadelphia.

Philadelphia's proud intellectual past proved an enormous help in achieving the city's renewal. The city's many great thinkers, inventors, and statesmen had already left behind quite a few educational legacies. Not the least of these was the University of Pennsylvania, another brainchild of Benjamin Franklin which quickly rose to Ivy League status and now boasts an illustrious list of alumni and an outstanding record of achievement in research and development.

Though they lack the University of Pennsylvania's pedigree, by elevating the educational mean of its citizens the many other Philadelphia-area colleges and universities have also contributed significantly to the elevation of the city in the twentieth century. They include Temple University, Drexel University, LaSalle University, St. Joseph's University, Philadelphia University, Bryn Mawr College, Haverford College, and Swarthmore College.

As the city took pains to beautify and better itself with bridges, roads, parks, and schools, some Philadelphia neighborhoods were made lovely simply by the passage of time. Looking very much like a Victorian town, Chestnut Hill features the best work of local architects in a breathtaking natural setting framed by Wissahickon Gorge and Cresheim Valley. The flowing waters of the Manayunk Canal, which once made the area a desirable site for factories, now add to the appeal of the neighborhood's classy restaurants, upscale stores, and posh

homes. In a similar twist of fate, overcrowded Chinatown learned to make the best of the constant immigration that once made that neighborhood squalid. Now, the steady flow of immigrants from the East is cherished as the source of the consistent authenticity of that area's shops, restaurants, and streets. South Street's rundown tenements and seedy parlors attracted all sorts of marginal characters in the '60s—and by the '70s the counterculture there had flourished into nothing less than an artistic renaissance. Today, the street's funky shops, cafés, tattoo parlors, bookstores, and crafts stores testify to that neighborhood's rebirth into modern, prosperous America.

And so was reborn all Philadelphia: Out of poverty came prosperity. Out of soot and smoke grew green parks and plazas. Out of countless different immigrant communities, one city with one future emerged.

Liberty Bell being moved on wagon with an escort of uniformed militia, circa 1903.

Poster promoting Port of Philadelphia, by Robert Muchley, 1937.

Where Past, Present, and Future Meet: Cultural Treasures

In the second half of the twentieth century, Philadelphians invested great amounts of time and energy in recovering and restoring their glorious past. Fortunately for those downtown, the largest project to do so also represented an extension of the city's efforts to relieve urban blight, this time bolstered by both state and federal support. Well aware of the American cultural treasures buried there, all levels of government united in the 1940s to remake the area around Independence Hall into a significant area of green space called Independence National Historic Park. The goal was to attract tourists to the area to learn about America's great legacy, to develop a sense of pride in her enduring natural treasures, and to nourish a sense of optimism about her future.

Establishment of the park began with demolition of eyesores and the erection of new institutions or the clearing of open space where they had stood. The Free Quaker Meeting House, constructed in 1783, was the only building left standing in the mall area to the north of Independence Hall. The national bicentennial celebration in 1976 provided a renewed motivation for improving Independence National Historic Park, and at that time the federal government gave the city another $30 million for related projects. To this day, development of the park remains an ongoing enterprise. The most recent additions are the National Constitution Center, an architectural triumph that offers interactive ways for visitors to learn about the Constitution, and a new home for the Liberty Bell, both of which were opened in 2003.

Also founded at the time of the bicentennial, the African-American Museum in Philadelphia became the nation's first city-financed museum dedicated to the history of African-Americans. Two other twentieth-century institutions reached back into history and pulled out new celebrations of Benjamin Franklin's ingenuity: The Fireman's Hall Museum acknowledges his citywide fire prevention campaign during the 1730s, which resulted in the formation of the colonies' first volunteer fire department in 1736. The Franklin Institute Science Museum honors Franklin by perpetuating his extensive interests in science and experimentation.

Even as Philadelphia was recapturing and reinventing its past, it provided for great future innovations through a variety of investments in the fine arts. The Avenue of the Arts, for example, a project begun in the 1990s to create an arts and entertainment district within the city, has both made the most of the area's existing art venues and added concert halls, theaters, clubs, and many special venues and events along Broad Street. One of the avenue's old jewels is the refurbished, 150-year-old Philadelphia Academy of Music, the nation's oldest grand opera house and one of the world's busiest performance halls. Nearby stands another longtime treasure, the Pennsylvania Academy of the Fine Arts, founded in 1805. A new gem on the avenue is the Kimmel Center for the Performing Arts, the new home to the renowned Philadelphia Orchestra, opened in 2001.

Of course, the Avenue of the Arts could not claim to be home to all of the city's art treasures. The Philadelphia Museum of Art, with hundreds of thousands of artworks, and the Rodin Museum both enrich the Benjamin Franklin Parkway.

In showing that it cherishes its history and has faith in its future, the city has actually managed to better accomplish recently some of the goals it set for itself decades ago: Cultural development has made it a stronger magnet for suburbanites, as well as for tourists from around the nation and even the world. At the same time, Center City's popularity as a residential area has begun to grow again—just like it did when William Penn gave it its first promise of freedom.

Houses of Worship and War: Remnants of Early American Life

The Schuylkill River

The 125-mile-long Schuylkill River is the largest tributary of the Delaware River, with a watershed that covers 2,100 square miles. To residents of Philadelphia, the Schuylkill River is what divides Center City from West Philadelphia, where the University of Pennsylvania is located.

Before Europeans arrived in the New World, Lenni Lenape Indians lived along the river. They fished, trapped, and farmed here year-round and, when summer came, traveled up the river to catch shad, which swim upstream to spawn. Because of waterfalls on the western border of what is now Philadelphia, these Indians called the river *Ganshowahanna*, "Falling Waters."

The first European known to explore the river was Arendt Corssen, who worked for the Dutch East India Company. He named the river *Schuyl Kil*, Dutch for "Hidden Creek," because dense vegetation almost completely hid the Schuylkill's confluence with the Delaware at League Island. The river first appeared on a map in 1644, when Peter Lindestrom drew New Sweden.

When William Penn began his colony, the Schuylkill was the best path into the interior of Pennsylvania. His hope was that colonists would settle the city from river to river (that is, from the east bank of the Schuylkill to the west bank of the Delaware), but Philadelphians crowded along the banks of the Delaware for more than a

Previous page: Old Fort Mifflin.

century. By the first half of the nineteenth century, the Schuylkill had a long array of wharves to receive coal shipments from canal boats, but locals still hadn't deemed it a desirable place to settle. In the latter half of that century, however, almost 200 years after Penn established the colony, Philadelphians finally began to fully populate the area closer to the Schuylkill. When the University of Pennsylvania made the leap across the river into West Philadelphia in the 1870s, it pretty much sealed the area's fate as a permanent site of settlement.

In 1695, thirty-nine Anglicans formed Christ Church, an enduring symbol of Philadelphia's historic importance to the nation. They bought land on Second Street and built a wooden church there a year later. The church became the spiritual home of many prominent Philadelphians in life, and its burial yard became their home in death.

Early in the eighteenth century, immigration rapidly increased the church's membership. As a result, members decided in 1729 to rebuild. By 1735, the new church's western half was completed as an addition to the old building. When the £3,000 project reached completion in 1744, the elegant finished product was widely recognized as an architectural showplace.

Although Anglicans did not approve of gambling, church leaders decided to use a lottery as well as subscriptions to collect enough money to build a steeple in 1754. The following year, eight bells were installed. It is said that the bells' first ringer died "by his ignorance and ill-judged management of the bell rope."

Christ Church played a pioneering role in helping the city's African-American population. In the 1730s, the church provided educational opportunities for young black men and women, some of whom underwent baptism. By 1744, the church's black communicants had asked to receive greater religious instruction, and so the church hired a "catechist to the Negroes." When the Bray Associates, led by English clergyman Thomas Bray, proposed establishing a school for African-Americans, the church hired a teacher to train about 30 young men and women.

In the third quarter of the eighteenth century, growing opposition to British policies divided the church as well as the colony. The rift began to grow in 1767, when Britain imposed the Townshend Acts, which placed high customs fees on many products. Some members joined boycotts of British goods, while others continued to buy them.

In 1774, the First Continental Congress met in Philadelphia to consider responses to the British government's series of harsh tax measures against the colonists, and Christ Church's assistant minister, Jacob Duché, assumed the role of chaplain to the Congress.

As the turmoil grew, the position of clergymen became increasingly troubled. Ministers within the Church of England take an oath in support of the king, hence Christ Church's

Benjamin Franklin burial site.

troops occupied the city, the church opened its doors to them. Duché continued to be unsure about the issue of independence and eventually returned to England. By 1779, backers of independence had gained control of the lay leadership and selected William White as rector of Christ Church and St. Peter's Church.

When George Washington became the nation's first president in 1889, he and his wife Martha rented a pew at Christ Church. Although the Washingtons belonged to an Anglican church in Virginia, when they were in Philadelphia they regularly attended Christ Church, where records show that Pew 69 was rented to "The President" during the 1790s.

Still standing on Market Street at Front, Christ Church, now designated as an Episcopal church, continues its tradition of reaching out to the neighborhood surrounding it. It has given special attention to the area's youngest residents, often offering food, education, and activities to poor children.

In addition, the Christ Church Burial Ground carries historic importance as the last resting place of more than 5,000 people, many of whom were important public figures. Benjamin Franklin, who was interred there less than a year after affixing his signature to the nation's new constitution, remains the most famous man in the cemetery. Others buried there include Benjamin Rush, a renowned physician; Richard Budden, who is often credited with bringing the Liberty Bell to America; Phillip Syng, the silversmith who designed the quill holder and inkstand utilized for the signing of the Declaration of Independence and the Constitution; and his grandson, Phillip Syng, the father of American surgery.

ministers and those of other Anglican churches had an obligation to back the British government's actions. Indeed, the city's Anglican clergy generally were against independence, although many acknowledged that Britain had violated the colonists' rights. Christ Church's rector, Richard Peters, even responded to Thomas Paine's revolutionary pamphlet *Common Sense* by writing a tract of his own. He called his work *Plain Truth*, and in it he opposed independence, arguing that England's constitution was the world's strongest. Despite their feelings, Christ Church's ministers agreed at the start of the war to take part in preaching to the militia.

Following approval of the Declaration of Independence on July 4, 1776, the church faced a choice between closing its doors and omitting prayers for the royal family from its services. The very same day, Duché, who had been named rector when Peters retired, turned to the church's committee of lay leaders for a decision on what the church should do in response to this dramatic change. The committee, which oversaw both Christ Church and St. Peter's Church, another Anglican congregation in Philadelphia, chose to eliminate the prayers and keep the churches open.

In the winter of 1777/1778, when British

Washington Square

Washington Square was one of the five public squares in William Penn's original street plan for the city, but it did not receive its name until 1825. That was a year of heightened patriotism in the country, and as a result of the nationalistic fervor the city decided to name the square in honor of George Washington.

In the colonial town's early years, the square was a popular spot for grazing animals because it had rich grass and a stream that ran through its northeast corner. Since that time, Washington Square has been utilized over and over again as a burial ground. Early on, it served as a potter's field for colonists whose families could not pay for a proper burial plot. During the American Revolution, more than 2,000 soldiers of the Continental Army were buried there, along with sailors and British prisoners. Some died from battle wounds, but many fell victim to diseases, such as camp fever and smallpox. Historians have speculated that Washington Square is the final resting place for more soldiers from that war than any other site in the country. Following the Revolution, victims of the city's yellow fever epidemics were buried there. The site was also used for camp meetings and cattle markets in the eighteenth and early nineteenth centuries. In 1815, the city hired French botanist François André Michaux to improve the grounds by planting a variety of trees in the square.

Beginning in the 1950s, a fundraising movement sought to revamp the square and to place a memorial to soldiers of the American Revolution there. The renovational design, which survives today, features diagonal paths that meet at a circular pool, and the addition of smaller trees and shrubs to emulate a colonial grove. The Tomb of the Unknown Soldier of the Revolution includes a 1922 bronze cast of a life-size statue of Washington by Jean-Antoine Houdon. At Washington's feet lies a sarcophagus that houses the remains of a Revolutionary soldier. A flame also was installed as part of the memorial.

Those who'd like to see something a little lighter at Washington Square should check out the sycamore that was added to the park at the time of the nation's bicentennial. Its seeds were taken to the moon by Apollo astronaut Stuart Roosa.

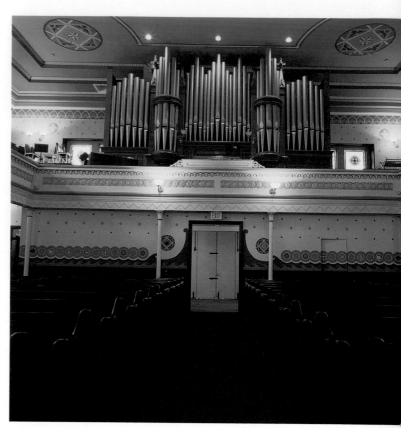

Old Pine Street Church and Churchyard

Old Pine Street Church is the oldest Presbyterian church in Philadelphia, completed in 1768 near the close of the colonial era. Located at 412 Pine Street, it stands on land granted to the church in 1764 by William Penn's sons, Thomas and Richard, "for the use of Presbyterians forever." In peaceful times, the church counted John Adams among its visitors, as well as Benjamin Rush, the well-known physician who encouraged Thomas Paine to write *Common Sense*. During the Revolutionary War, the church was led by an ardent Patriot, George Duffield, who served as chaplain to the Continental Congress and to Pennsylvania's militia. When the British occupied Philadelphia, the army used the church as a military hospital and stable, and soldiers used the wooden pews as firewood.

More than 3,000 graves can be found in the adjacent churchyard. Among those buried on the site are four renowned figures: William Hurry, Colonel William Linnard, General John Steele, and Thomas Brainerd. Hurry is traditionally credited with ringing the Liberty Bell after the first public reading of the Declaration of Independence. In the Battle of Germantown in 1777, Linnard ordered the placement of a cannon at the mouth of Wissahickon Creek, where it fired upon Hessian troops. Steele was George Washington's aide-de-camp and accompanied him at Yorktown, Virginia, where Great Britain's Charles Cornwallis surrendered to Patriot forces in 1781. Brainerd was a leader of the anti-slavery movement and the church's sixth pastor. In addition, 300 Hessian troops were buried in the churchyard during the Revolutionary War.

In the middle of the nineteenth century, the church underwent major reconstruction. Corinthian columns were paired beneath its newly elevated roof, transforming the once-Georgian structure into a striking piece of Greek Revival architecture. Today, the church is still plenty active and welcomes visitors from near and far.

Mikveh Israel Cemetery

Mikveh Israel Synagogue on at 44 North Fourth Street is home to Philadelphia's oldest Jewish cemetery. In 1956, the cemetery received designation as a National Historic Shrine and became part of Independence National Historic Park.

The first Jews came to what is now Philadelphia in the mid-seventeenth century, when the area was under Dutch control. Those early arrivals did not establish a community, but simply traded with Indians. Among the first Jews to settle here was Nathan Levy, a merchant who moved to Philadelphia from New York. Less than a year after he moved here, one of his children died, and Levy established a private burial ground on Walnut Street. In 1740, he set up a permanent cemetery on Spruce Street between Eighth and Ninth Streets. At that time, William Penn's son, Thomas, ordered that the land be held in trust as a burial place for Jews. Twelve years later, Levy received an additional plot of land to expand the cemetery, and its area was increased yet again in 1765. The deed to that site passed into the hands of Mikveh Israel Synagogue in 1774. Congregation Mikveh Israel named five trustees for the burial ground in 1791 and produced a document stating the congregation's intention to make the cemetery available as a burial site to any Jews in Philadelphia.

Today, the tomb of Levy, who died in 1753, carries the oldest readable inscription in the tiny historic cemetery. Other prominent Jews buried in the Mikveh Israel Cemetery include pioneer Aaron Levy; Rebecca Gratz, who founded and led several social and educational organizations during the nineteenth century; and Benjamin Nones, who served on the staffs of George Washington and the Marquis de Lafayette. The burial ground also contains two plaques honoring Haym Salomon, a broker who contributed to the Patriots' battle in the American Revolution.

Head House Square

In its early days, Philadelphia's market days were Wednesdays and Saturdays, and its marketplace was located on High Street. (High Street was later renamed Market Street, because the people had always called it that regardless of its official name.) As the market became increasingly crowded, the marketplace spread westward on High Street. In 1745, a new market was established just south of the old one. Originally, it was logically called New Market, but later its name was changed to Head House Square—which makes very little sense today, considering there's nothing square at all about this oblong island in the middle of Second Street.

When it was built, the market stood between rows of brick houses, where cabinetmakers, blacksmiths, bakers, merchants, and ship captains lived. Many of the tradesmen had shops underneath their homes fronting on the square, and merchants once set up stalls in the market's brick arcade. In 1803, a small, attractive Georgian building topped by a cupola and weathervane was added at the square's north end to serve as home and workplace for the market's master, who checked the quality of goods and tried to guarantee the legitimacy of sales.

From its early days as a colonial marketplace all the way up until today, Head House Square, in one way or another, has served people with items to sell. It was restored in the 1960s after Mayor Richardson Dilworth stepped forward and urged the city to preserve its only surviving colonial marketplace. Since then, it is often used on summer weekends by artists and craftsmen who sell their wares to tourists.

In a neighborhood filled with warehouses, shops, restaurants, and galleries, the little road known as Elfreth's Alley claims the distinction of being the United States' oldest continuously occupied residential street. Walking down the narrow street, as thousands of tourists do each year, is like moving through the past. Thirty-three houses, most built before the American Revolution, stand alongside the cobblestones. All but one of them remains a private residence.

Arthur Wells, a blacksmith, and John Gilbert, a bolter, opened the alley in 1702. It began as little more than a cartway for merchants transporting goods from Second Street to Front Street, where the products were loaded onto ships. The tiny street runs parallel to and between Arch and Race Streets.

The alley was named for Jeremiah Elfreth, a blacksmith working on Second Street who built the alley's first house in 1713. Other homes soon

Typical house on Elfreth's Alley.

were crowded into the small roadway, the earliest of which probably were made of wood. Many served as both a home and a business, as blacksmiths, nailsmiths, and locksmiths often used the first floor for business, while their families lived on the upper floors.

In Elfreth's Alley today, two of the street's original houses still stand. Thought to have been built between 1725 and 1727, they are twin houses connected by a passageway. One of these houses belonged to the tanner Andrew Edge, the other to Thomas Potts, who rented the house to tenants. After the houses had been built and occupied, Edge was surprised to learn in 1728 that he had built a house on Potts' lot and Potts had constructed one on his. As a result, the two landowners took the necessary measures to exchange deeds.

Edge's house was later occupied by two of his married daughters and their husbands. When Mary Edge's husband was lost in a privateering venture, she advertised the house for sale in the *Pennsylvania Gazette*. The 1759 advertisement described it as "very convenient for any Person that follows the Water." Potts' house was rented by a series of tenants. The first was William Maudridge, a ship joiner and carpenter. Others included Joseph Hill, who made his living as a sea captain, pilot, and oysterman.

In the mid-eighteenth century, Jeremiah Elfreth was the street's biggest property owner and land-lord. He often rented tiny abodes to sea captains and shipwrights, but he also found a variety of artisans among his lessees. Included among them were cordwainers, carvers, bakers, potters, pewter workers, tailors, boatbuilders, joiners, coopers, and furniture makers. In 1762, Elfreth sold one house to a Quaker named Israel Cassell, the shipwright who later was responsible for detaining American ships that attempted to evacuate Philadelphia when the British army occupied the city during the American Revolution.

Adam Clampfer, a shopkeeper, constructed two homes on the alley that he rented out to tenants. In another building on the street he kept

his store and tavern, where he sold molasses, New England rum, and West Indian hogheads.

From 1749 through 1751, Elfreth's Alley acquired a new extension bit by bit as a cobblestone path named Bladen's Court was built. It ultimately provided access to five houses, and a water pump and outdoor privies were installed in the court for the convenience of the residents. The last house to be built on the alley, house number 125, was constructed in 1836 and is the street's only four-story building.

One house on the little street was purchased by two sisters-in-law who made a living sewing mantuas, loosely fitting gowns worn by seventeenth- and eighteenth-century women. Today,

Mantua Makers House at 126 Elfreth's Alley is the Elfreth's Alley Museum. The three-story home features period furniture on the first floor; on the second, visitors can see photos showing the interiors of several preserved houses on the alley; and the third floor houses a bedroom with period furniture. In the backyard is planted a colonial garden.

The Elfreth's Alley Home and Garden Tour is held each year on the second weekend in June. On this Saturday and Sunday, alley residents dress in colonial garb and welcome visitors to the street, and handmade goods and traditional foods are sold to raise money for preservation of the street.

Stenton

James Logan, secretary to Pennsylvania's founder William Penn, built and resided in this Georgian mansion on 500 acres of land near Germantown Road. Completed around 1730, Stenton served Logan as a grand country house: it included a privy, icehouse, barn, Colonial Revival garden, and a kitchen wing.

In 1699, at the age of only 25, Logan joined Penn on a voyage from England to America. When Penn returned home, Logan stayed behind as his representative and helped to manage the colony over the next fifty years.

Like Penn, Logan was a Quaker and a man of broad knowledge and sophistication. He developed a personal library of almost 3,000 books, which later became part of the Library Company of Philadelphia's collection. His great love of reading was noted by Benjamin Franklin, who said that "[h]is life was for the most part a life of business, tho' he had always been passionately fond of study."

After his death in 1751, James' son William Logan took over Stenton's ownership. With a house in the center of the city as his primary residence, Stenton was for him primarily a summer home. William died in 1776 and his son, George Logan, inherited the house. He left Stenton unused during most of the American Revolution, although it served as a military headquarters at various times in October 1777 for both George Washington and his adversary, Sir William Howe. Howe was at Stenton when he first heard of Washington's surprise attack in the Battle of Germantown, in which the British triumphed.

In 1781, George Logan married Deborah Norris, a neighbor and historian, who was among the first to hear the Declaration of Independence read. George became a doctor, and the couple lived in the house for forty years. In 1910, the house was purchased by the city, which later restored it. Today, Stenton is a stunning architectural showplace furnished with many pieces of the Logans' original furniture.

Old City Tavern

In 1772, a group of leading businessmen, including one descendant of William Penn, agreed upon plans to create an upscale tavern to serve the most populous city in the colonies and its many visitors. These well-to-do men managed to establish "the most convenient and elegant structure of its Kind in America."

The City Tavern was built in 1773 and opened late that same year at Second and Walnut Streets. It offered lodgings to travelers and, most notably, to delegates attending the First and Second Continental Congresses. The five-floor tavern also became a popular hub for interactions between traders and political leaders.

However, the tavern's owners wanted to make it more than a place of business—they sought to make it a center of the community. To that end, they invited local societies to meet there in a variety of well-decorated, spacious rooms with lofty ceilings. During the First Continental Congress, as many as 500 men attended one such gathering, and in 1787 the tavern hosted the Constitutional Convention's closing banquet. Future president John Adams, who had visited the best taverns of New York and Boston, called the City Tavern "the most genteel one in America."

The tavern was never properly renovated after it was damaged by a fire in 1834 and, despite its rich history, was demolished in 1854. One newspaper reported that it had been "immolated on the altar of improvement." Today, a reconstruction of the tavern stands at Second and Walnut Streets and serves cuisine typical of the eighteenth century.

Franklin Court

Benjamin Franklin, who moved from Boston to Philadelphia in 1723 at the age of 17, quickly became widely known as a printer, as publisher of the *Pennsylvania Gazette*, and as the witty writer of *Poor Richard's Almanac*. He founded the first circulating library in 1731, and five years later led a fire-prevention drive that spurred the formation of Philadelphia's first fire company. In 1737, he assumed the profitable position of Philadelphia's postmaster. He then turned his attention to education and, in 1742, proposed the creation of what became the University of Pennsylvania. Ten years later, Franklin created the first American fire insurance company, and he became the first president of the American Philosophical Society in 1769.

Franklin made considerable contributions as well to the causes of independence and liberty. He participated in the Second Continental Congress in 1776 and the Constitutional Convention in 1787, and he helped to negotiate the peace treaty ending hostilities with Great Britain. He was also head of the Pennsylvania Society for Promoting the Abolition of Slavery.

Beginning in 1763, Benjamin Franklin oversaw construction of a three-story brick home for his family on Market Street between Third and Fourth Streets. Two years later, while Franklin served in London as Pennsylvania's representative in dealings with the royal government, his wife, Deborah, moved the family into its new home. The family remained there for the rest of Franklin's life, though he often lived in Europe as a representative of the colony and later of the new nation. Franklin died in the home in 1790 at the age of 84. In the early 1800s, the city's residential area was moving further west, and Franklin's house was in the heart of the business district. Citizens of the United States were not very history-conscious in those days, and so, in 1812, the house was simply torn down to make room for a business.

When Philadelphians began trying to restore much of the city's eighteenth-century past, too little was known about Franklin's home and his adjacent print shop to make a true re-creation possible. As a result, a modern monument to him was erected instead, consisting of a simple steel framework at the location of his home.

Left: Franklin Court Post Office and Book Store.

Opposite: Steel framework at the location of Benjamin Franklin's home.

Betsy Ross House

Betsy Ross, a seamstress, long has been credited with creating the first American flag at the time of the American Revolution, and 239 Arch Street is purportedly the place where she did it. The brick house has become a popular tourist destination known as the Betsy Ross House.

Betsy Griscom broke with her Quaker family when she married John Ross, an Episcopalian, in 1773, and together they started a flag and upholstery company. Just three years after joining the Pennsylvania militia, John was killed in a munitions explosion. After his death, Betsy returned to Quakerism, but as a Free Quaker, or "Fighting Quaker," who supported the Patriots' cause in the battle for freedom from England.

According to tradition, Betsy used her sewing skills in her family's upholstery and flag business. In 1776, a committee of the Second Continental Congress reportedly asked her to produce a flag of red, white, and blue that featured thirteen stars and thirteen stripes, representing the original states. As the story goes, that committee included George Washington as well as her husband's uncle, George Ross.

Modern historians believe the story of Ross's connection to the flag is a myth created in the late nineteenth century by her grandson, William J. Canby. Early in the twentieth century, a book called *The Evolution of the American Flag*, written by Canby's brother and nephew, attracted new attention to the legend. Subsequently, money was raised through ten-cent contributions to preserve the house, and the American Flag House and Betsy Ross Memorial Association was incorporated. Scholars are not even sure that Ross lived in the house that now carries her name. She may have rented rooms at 241 Arch Street.

Nevertheless, what is popularly known as the Betsy Ross House is at least a good example of typical architecture of Ross's period. Constructed around 1760, the 2.5-story home has narrow, winding stairs, a gabled roof, and eight rooms, including a kitchen in the basement. The American Flag House and Betsy Ross Memorial Association, which runs the museum, has placed Ross's reading glasses and period furniture in the home as well, creating an authentic eighteenth-century atmosphere.

Ross outlived two husbands before dying at the age of 84 in 1836. She is buried in Atwater Kent Park next to the Betsy Ross House.

Graff House

The Graff House, now standing at the corner of Seventh and Market Streets in Center City Philadelphia, is a reconstruction of the building once owned by Jacob Graff Jr. When the 33-year-old Thomas Jefferson attended the Second Continental Congress in Philadelphia, he rented two rooms from Graff, and it was there that he wrote his drafts of the Declaration of Independence.

Jefferson, John Adams, Robert R. Livingston, Roger Sherman, and Benjamin Franklin had been chosen to formulate a declaration of the colonies' grievances against the British monarch and their plans to fight for freedom. The bulk of the work fell upon Jefferson, a delegate representing the colony of Virginia. In the days when the intersection of Seventh and Market Streets was still on the outskirts of town, Jefferson found quiet time to work in Graff's house. He later wrote: "At the time of writing that instrument I

was lodged in the house of a Mr. Gratz [Graff], a new brick house, three stories high, of which I rented the second floor. . . . In that parlor I wrote habitually, and in it wrote that paper [the Declaration of Independence] particularly."

The Graff House was just a year old when Jefferson stayed there. That original house, a Georgian brick building heated by many fireplaces, was torn down in 1883 and replaced with a bank building. Eighty-five years later, the Philadelphia Convention and Visitors Bureau allocated $2 million to rebuild the house using old photographs. Completed in 1975, the replica is now a part of Independence National Historic Park. It includes two stone lintels from the original building as well as period furniture and reproductions installed to recapture the era in which Jefferson worked.

Bartram's Garden

Bartram's Garden is the United States' oldest botanical garden. Encompassing forty-five acres, the garden represents what is left of the original 102-acre farm used as a showcase for rare plants by John Bartram, a Quaker farmer who became royal botanist to King George III. Bartram constructed his stone residence along the Schuylkill River with his own hands between 1728 and 1731, then expanded it in 1770. After Bartram died in 1777, his son William maintained the nursery until 1850.

James Logan, William Penn's representative in the colonies, nurtured the elder Bartram's interest in botany. Bartram traveled as far north as Canada and as far south as Florida in his quest for plants, many of which were kept in his garden, while others were shipped to England. In 1751, Bartram published *Observations on the Inhabitants, Climate, Soil, etc. . . . made by John Bartram in his travels from Pennsilvania to Lake Ontario*, an account of a trip taken in 1743.

Today, Bartram's land is a part of Fairmount Park. The garden encompasses the Bartram family house, a botanical garden, meadows, parkland, and a wetland. In all, more than 100 trees and shrubs associated with Bartram are on display. English oak, pine, fir trees, and boxwoods in the garden date back to shipments from the Earl of Bute to Bartram in the late eighteenth century. Particularly special is the *Franklinia alatamaha* tree, which was discovered by Bartram and his son during a 1765 trip to Georgia. On a later trip, William gathered seeds of the tree and named it in honor of his father's friend, Benjamin Franklin. The tree has not been spotted in the wild since 1803.

Benjamin Franklin National Memorial

In the year of the nation's bicentennial, Pennsylvania dedicated the Benjamin Franklin National Memorial in the rotunda of Memorial Hall, a chamber in the Franklin Institute Science Museum that was opened in 1938. Sculpted by James Earle Fraser, the towering marble statue weighs thirty tons and stands twenty feet high atop a ninety-two-ton pedestal of white Seravezza marble.

Fraser was born in Winona, Minnesota, in 1876. Included among his other works are two Washington landmarks: a 1921 statue of Alexander Hamilton that stands in front of the United States Treasury, and the southern pediment at the National Archives Building, dedicated in 1935. Fraser's most renowned work is the 1915 sculpture *The End of the Trail*, depicting a weary Indian on horseback. The artist also designed the buffalo nickel, which the U.S. Mint produced from 1913 until 1938.

Fraser's work is well showcased in Memorial Hall. Inspired by Rome's Pantheon, architect John T. Windrim designed the hall eighty-two feet in height, length, and width, with a self-supporting domed ceiling weighing 1,600 tons. The hall also showcases some of Franklin's possessions, including scientific experiments and an odometer that Franklin used to measure postal routes in Philadelphia during his service as the city's postmaster. To keep Franklin's spirit of innovation alive, the Benjamin Franklin National Memorial bestows annual awards for substantial contributions to business and science.

Pennsylvania Hospital

The oldest hospital in the United States is Pennsylvania Hospital in Philadelphia. Like many Philadelphia institutions, the hospital traces its roots to Benjamin Franklin. At a time when doctors cared almost exclusively for the wealthy in their homes, Franklin united with Dr. Thomas Bond and others to found a community hospital that would care for the poor. Franklin's ingenuity paid off when he convinced the Pennsylvania Assembly to contribute £2,000 if the project's backers could solicit a matching amount—an easy task for someone with Franklin's connections. (Interestingly, this may be the very first example of matching government and private funds in the colonies.) After taking care of the operation's finances, he served on the institution's first board of managers and was its first secretary and second president.

Initially, the hospital opened temporary headquarters on the southeast corner of Fifth and High (Market) Streets, where the first patients were admitted on February 10, 1752. To manage day-to-day operations, the hospital's leaders had hired a matron to "govern the Family and nurse the Sick," a man to oversee the insane patients, and one nurse. Six physicians served the hospital in its first year—including Thomas Bond and his brother, Phineas—each making a required two visits a week. The doctors donated whatever medicines were needed throughout the first year; after that, hospital income allowed the doctors to order medicines from England and to open a public apothecary, which itself became a source of income. In December 1756, the hospital moved to its current site north of Pine between Eighth and Ninth Streets.

Left: The Hospital gardens.

Opposite: The William Penn statue, which can be seen in the center of the Pine Building's front lawn and was donated by John Penn, William's grandson. He discovered the statue in a London antique shop and presented it to the hospital in 1804, the same year the Pine Center Building was completed.

Additional buildings were added to the site in 1796 and 1804.

Pennsylvania Hospital is now part of the University of Pennsylvania Hospital System. The University of Pennsylvania has an interesting medical history of its own: It established the continent's first school of medicine in 1765, and the Hospital of the University of Pennsylvania was formed in 1874. The university continues to pride itself on its medical innovations: over the last thirty years, physicians and scientists at Penn have introduced total intravenous feeding, developed the first general vaccine for pneumonia, and created magnetic resonance imaging (MRI).

Evidence of the institution's role as one of the nation's medical leaders is found in Pennsylvania Hospital's many interesting historical exhibits. In addition to a historic library and displays of early medical instruments, there is a surgical amphitheater, where operations were performed from 1804 to 1868. During that time period, doctors limited themselves to amputations, repairs of aneurysms, and extractions of tumors, stones, and cataracts. The hospital also houses the Museum of Nursing History and a portrait gallery. The artist Benjamin West donated his 1817 painting *Christ Healing the Sick in the Temple* to the hospital, where it hangs in the Gallery Pavilion. When it was first hung, Philadelphians flocked to the hospital, eager to pay the admission for a chance to see it.

The Pine Street side of the hospital grounds is park-like. It includes a garden of therapeutic herbs and an eighteenth-century lead statue of William Penn by an unknown artist, purchased from a London junk dealer by Penn's grandson, John, and donated to the hospital. Also on the grounds is the unmarked grave of Mary Girard, wife of one of the nineteenth century's wealthiest Americans, Stephen Girard.

Cliveden

Cliveden, often called "the Chew House," is an elegant colonial home on over six acres of land. It was built by Benjamin Chew during the 1760s. Chew wanted a fine townhouse as his "country seat," and indeed, his home in the Germantown neighborhood of Philadelphia, then a suburban village, became one of the grandest houses in the American colonies. The main house had a symmetrical facade, and local laborers skillfully cut native stones, reducing the sizes of the blocks from foundation to roof in order to make the house appear taller. Chew decorated the interior lavishly and named his new home after the country estate of Frederick, Prince of Wales.

Both Chew's life and his home were significantly altered by the Revolutionary War. He served as chief justice of colonial Pennsylvania's Supreme Court and refused to give up that royal appointment when colonists began to seek independence. Apparently because of his closeness to the Penn family and his political stands, some saw him as a Loyalist, and as a result, he spent a year of the war under house arrest in New Jersey. In the aftermath of that ordeal, he maintained a low profile until the war had ended.

The carriage house at Cliveden.

His house, however, became a focal point of the American Revolution on October 4, 1777. After George Washington and his troops marched on Germantown, about 125 surprised British troops took refuge in the house. Washington ordered a full attack on the house, but after hours of cannon- and musket-fire, the Patriot forces withdrew. They had lost about seventy-seven men, while only two or three British soldiers had died inside. Many of the dead were buried on the Chew property later that day.

After the battle, Chew repaired the house and sold it. When the war ended, though, Chew was able to regain his position of prominence in the community, and he repurchased Cliveden in 1797. With the exception of that brief interruption, seven generations of his family dwelled there over the course of two centuries, until ownership was transferred to the National Trust for Historic Preservation in 1972. Today, the historic house museum contains artifacts from the Revolutionary period and is open to the public.

Independence Hall

Independence Hall, where the Declaration of Independence and Constitution were ratified, is unquestionably Philadelphia's most historic building. Its history began simply, when the Pennsylvania Assembly voted in 1729 to build a state house. Construction started in 1732 on Chestnut Street between Fifth and Sixth Streets, but the building was not ready for occupancy until 1741. People began calling the State House "Independence Hall" in the nineteenth century, although its official name was not changed until the next century. Philadelphians today would probably be confused if they actually heard Independence Hall called "the State House," even though that was originally its official name.

The State House played a vital role in the blossoming cultural life of the city. It served as a temporary home for the Library Company of Philadelphia, the city's first subscription library, and it hosted scientists who used its rooms for experiments in electricity and experimental philosophy.

With the approach of the American Revolution, the State House Yard became a popular gathering place for disgruntled colonists and a forum for popular debate on how to respond to the imposition of new taxes. In 1774, unhappy colonists began calling for a general congress of all of the colonies. Inside the State House, Governor John Penn managed to kill the proposal. However, a different story unfolded outside. On June 18, thousands rallied in the State House Yard, resulting in recommendations that a colonial congress be convened.

The First Continental Congress was held at Carpenters' Hall in Philadelphia in the fall of 1774. Shortly thereafter, the Second Continental Congress came to Philadelphia in May 1775 and met in the State House. Though fighting with the British had already begun, colonial leaders were still far from united on the question of independence. Nevertheless, on May 10, the delegates unanimously chose George Washington to lead

Continental forces in protecting the rights of colonists. Exactly one year after Washington's election, the Continental Congress approved a resolution requiring all colonies to set up a government that was free of British oversight.

In June 1776, a committee of the Continental Congress assigned Thomas Jefferson to write the Declaration of Independence. On July 1, the Congress voted and approved Jefferson's work. On July 4, the colonial representatives amended the document and then approved it as "the unanimous Declaration of the Thirteen United States of America." Four days later, Sheriff John Nixon read the declaration to a crowd in the State House Yard, and that evening members of the crowd tore down the king's coat of arms from the State House courtroom and burned it.

The Second Continental Congress met at the State House until the British occupied Philadelphia in 1777. For several months before their departure, the British used the State House as a prison for captured American officers, but eventually the lawmakers returned to their old home. Two months after the British finally surrendered in October 1781, the victorious Washington—welcomed by adoring crowds in the streets of Philadelphia—came to speak to the Pennsylvania General Assembly in the State House.

Over the years, as the newly independent colonies tried to govern under the Articles of Confederation, the articles' preventative measures against the formation of a strong central government created considerable diplomatic and financial difficulties for them. This trouble finally led to a 1787 national convention in the State House, with Washington presiding. The Constitutional Convention, as this meeting came to be called, began May 25 and ran into September. Ultimately, the delegates agreed on a strong federal government, but they still implemented safeguards against tyranny, such as the establishment of a two-house legislature and the separation of powers between the executive, the legislative, and the judiciary.

In 1790, the federal government moved from New York to Philadelphia to await the construction of Washington, D.C. While here, Congress made its home at Congress Hall instead of Independence Hall. In 1799, the Pennsylvania state government also left the State House behind, moving the capital westward toward its eventual home in Harrisburg. Having lost its governmental purpose, the structure was converted into a museum for the artist Charles Willson Peale in 1802. Fourteen years later, the State House was suddenly threatened with demolition to make room for new buildings. In order to guarantee that it would be preserved, the city bought the historic site in 1818.

The 1824 visit of the Marquis de Lafayette, a hero of the American Revolution, reconfigured the State House in public memory. When Lafayette visited the meeting room where the Declaration of Independence was finalized, he proclaimed: "Here within these sacred walls . . .

Assembly Hall.

Carpenters' Hall, which hosted the First Continental Congress in 1774 and was home to Benjamin Franklin's Library Company, The American Philosophical Society, and the First and Second Banks of the United States.

was boldly declared the independence of these United States. Here, sir, was planned the formation of our virtuous, brave, Revolutionary army and the providential inspiration received that gave the command of it to our beloved, matchless Washington." From this time forward, the State House increasingly became known as Independence Hall.

Over the years, presidents from Abraham Lincoln to John F. Kennedy have spoken at Independence Hall, and the historical site has provided a forum for public protests on many issues, including the rights of African-Americans, the importance of environmentalism, and opposition to the Vietnam War. In the mid-twentieth century, Independence Hall fell under the auspices of the National Parks Service. To create Independence National Historic Park, some less significant eighteenth- and nineteenth-century buildings were demolished, opening up a mall of open space and historical institutions for celebration of the city's beginnings.

The Liberty Bell

The Liberty Bell plays a central role in the history and traditions of Philadelphia. State officials ordered production of the bell in 1751 to mark the fiftieth anniversary of the colony's Charter of Privileges, in which William Penn granted colonists of Pennsylvania many rights not enjoyed by residents of other colonies. The words to be inscribed on the bell were selected by the speaker of the Pennsylvania Assembly, Isaac Norris Jr., who chose a simple message from the Book of Leviticus: "Proclaim liberty throughout all the land to all the inhabitants thereof."

The bell, manufactured at Whitechapel Foundry in England, reached Philadelphia in the fall of 1752. Unfortunately, it cracked the first time it was rung. Two local foundry workers melted it down and recast it, adding more than an ounce of copper to make it less brittle. When that work was done, officials were dissatisfied with the tone of the new bell, and so it once again was broken and recast. Finally, in March 1753, it was hung in the belfry of the State House, which later became known as Independence Hall.

Officials ordered the ringing of the bell to mark many important events, including Benjamin Franklin's departure for England to present the colonists' grievances to the Crown, the coronation of George III, and the opening of the meetings at which citizens debated responses to the Sugar Act in 1764 and the Stamp Act in 1765. In fact, the bell rang so many times that neighbors complained. They sent a petition to the State Assembly in 1772 to report that they were "incommoded and distressed" by the frequent "ringing of the great Bell in the steeple." A 1774 account also stated that the steeple was in such a state of disrepair that there was some concern about ringing the bell.

According to popular tradition, the bell rang again on July 4, 1776, to announce approval of the Declaration of Independence and to mark the birth of a new nation. However, that story does not appear in contemporary accounts, but rather emerged years later in the writings of George Lippard in the mid-nineteenth century. We do know that some city bells rang July 8, 1776, to celebrate the declaration's first reading. That the Liberty Bell was among them is somewhat doubtful because of the dilapidated nature of the steeple.

The Liberty Bell's most well-documented role in the American Revolution may have been its removal as the British army prepared to occupy Philadelphia in 1777. Along with other bells from the city, it was stashed away under the floorboards of Zion Reformed Church in Allentown until the occupying army had left the city.

From 1790 to 1799, when Philadelphia served as the center of government for both the United States and the state of Pennsylvania, the bell rang for various purposes: it alerted state legislators that a session was about to begin, called voters to turn in their ballots at the State House, and became part of celebrations to mark George Washington's birthday and the Fourth of July.

There is disagreement about when the bell

Liberty Bell Center.

originally suffered its famous crack. It is certain that the crack expanded to the point of making the bell unusable during the 1846 celebration that marked the anniversary of Washington's birth. By the mid-1850s, the bell had been removed from the tower and placed on a pedestal in Independence Hall. The pedestal's inscription recounted its reported role in announcing approval of the Declaration of Independence.

Over the years, the Liberty Bell gained symbolism as a representation of American freedom. In 1837, the bell became a symbol of a new struggle for liberty when abolitionists adopted it as a frontispiece in *Liberty*, a publication of the New York Anti-Slavery Society. Years later, when the battle over slavery had been resolved, the Liberty Bell went on the road to promote liberty across the United States. It made seven railroad journeys between 1885 and 1915, attracting the attention of huge crowds at World's Fairs and other exhibitions. It also played

a key role in the largely unsuccessful sesquicentennial celebration of the Declaration of Independence in Philadelphia in 1926: a gigantic, eighty-foot-high replica of the bell towered over Broad Street, brightly illuminated by 26,000 lightbulbs. Designers were careful to allow enough room for cars to pass beneath it.

The bell was moved to a home of its own on Independence Mall in 1976, when the nation celebrated its bicentennial. Given the fact that it probably did not ring on July 4, 1776, its historic credentials are somewhat questionable, but tourists to the mall see the bell as a symbol of freedom nevertheless. It is now housed in the Liberty Bell Center, which was opened on Independence Mall in October 2003. Each July Fourth, youngsters descended from the signers of the Declaration of Independence tap the bell thirteen times as bells across the nation ring thirteen times in unison, symbolizing the thirteen original colonies' decision to seek independence.

Gloria Dei Church

Gloria Dei Church, also known as Old Swedes' Church, is the oldest church in Pennsylvania. The church's founders were early Swedish settlers who came to the Philadelphia area years before William Penn received a land grant from the English government. Surrounded by trees and its pastoral graveyard, Gloria Dei Church remains an oasis in an urban environment.

Established in 1646, the congregation originally met on Tinicum Island. Around 1677, its members began gathering in a log blockhouse at Wicaco, a settlement in what is now South Philadelphia. By 1700, a new church had been built on the south end of the growing settlement of Philadelphia, where it still stands at what is now 916 South Swanson Street. When built, the church actually stood very close to the Delaware River's edge. Over the years, however, land accumulation along the shore has narrowed the river, and so the church seems distant from the river today. The church has also grown distant from its origins, as well: As its members became anglicized, they left behind their Swedish and Lutheran roots and transformed Gloria Dei into an Episcopal church, which it remains today.

In addition to being the city's oldest house of worship, Gloria Dei was the scene of the city's first music recital in 1703, when Justus Falckner was ordained. The church was also the site of one of Betsy Ross's three marriages. Among the fascinating treasures within the church are a 1608 Bible and wood carvings salvaged from the original church, which was destroyed by fire. Suspended from the ceiling are hangings that depict two ships that brought Swedes to the area.

Notably, the churchyard holds the grave of the first man to popularize bird-watching in America, Alexander Wilson. There's also a monument to the first president of the United States, the often-forgotten John Hanson, who held office in 1781 and 1782, while the nation was governed by the Articles of Confederation.

Thaddeus Kosciuszko Statue

Born in Poland, Thaddeus Kosciuszko arrived in Philadelphia in 1776. He was moved to tears when he read the Declaration of Independence for the first time, and he journeyed to Virginia to meet its author, Thomas Jefferson. Later, he offered his services to George Washington and the Continental Congress and, in October 1776, received the commission of colonel of engineers.

He immediately started to work fortifying potential battle sites. Among his first priorities was a strengthening of defenses on the Philadelphia waterfront and at Fort Mercer in New Jersey. Later he was sent to New York, where he helped build fortifications on the Hudson River and mapped out strategies for the defense of Saratoga. In 1778, he became chief engineer of West Point. Five years later, Washington named him brigadier general and honored him with the Cincinnati Order medal.

Engulfed in the revolutionary spirit, Kosciuszko decided to return to his homeland in 1784, where he was among the leaders of a failed revolt against the Russians, who were occupying Poland at the time. He suffered seventeen injuries in the 1794 Battle of Maciejowice and was eventually captured. In 1796, he received amnesty under the condition that he leave Poland and never return. Kosciuszko accepted that condition and, in 1797, once again found himself in Philadelphia, where he received a hero's welcome. He moved into a boarding house at Third and Pine Streets, which is now a museum bearing his name. The following year he set out for Europe again, where he lived the rest of his life in Switzerland. Kosciuszko was buried in Krakow, Poland, in Wawel Castle—where Polish kings were laid to rest.

Today, Philadelphia remembers Kosciuszko on the Benjamin Franklin Parkway in a statue by Marian Konieczny. The statue was a gift given to the city's residents by the Polish people in 1976, the year of the United States' bicentennial.

George Washington's headquarters. General Washington rented this house, owned by Isaac Potts, from its occupant, Mrs. Deborah Hewes. Here the general and his staff received local officials and foreign dignitaries, in addition to coordinating the daily operations of the entire continental army.

When the British army occupied Philadelphia, Patriot soldiers made camp at Valley Forge, about twenty-two miles northwest of the city. The Continental Army took a defensive stand in the hills, where soldiers were well positioned to stop any attack the British might launch against the temporary U.S. capital in York or the local supply depot near Reading. At this historic site George Washington and his troops survived the infamous winter of 1777/1778, in which they suffered cold, hunger, and disease.

At Valley Forge, soldiers found water in abundance and plentiful wood to burn and to use in constructing shelters. However, food was another matter. Local farmers shared some of their crops, but by the middle of winter, many

soldiers were approaching starvation. The troops reported a diet of "fire cakes and cold water." (Fire cakes were made by mixing flour and water, then frying the batter on a griddle.) Some also lacked clothing to protect them from the elements, and the men lived in groups of twelve in cold, wet, smoky log huts with dirt floors and sheets of cloth for doors.

The Marquis de Lafayette, a French member of Washington's staff, described the miserable scene: "The unfortunate soldiers were in want in everything; they had neither coats nor hats, nor shirts, nor shoes. Their feet and their legs froze until they were black, and it was often necessary to amputate them." Gouverneur Morris, a member of the Continental Congress, reported, "An Army of skeletons appeared before our eyes naked, starved, sick and discouraged."

Washington accused the Congress of indifference to their plight. "I feel superabundantly for them," he wrote, "and from my soul pity those miseries, which it is neither in my power to relieve or prevent." The problem was not a lack of supplies—the supplies existed. However, the army was unable to transport those supplies to Valley Forge. Roads were poor, and the low value of Continental currency made it difficult to hire drivers.

Replicated hut, Mulhenberg Brigade. Washington had his troops build log cabins to get through the winter at Valley Forge because they could be constructed rapidly and inexpensively and were substantially weatherproof.

Not surprisingly, disease struck many men. Dysentery and typhus were common because of poor sanitation, partially caused by the rotting carcasses of horses. Washington also was forced to issue an order that any man who relieved himself anywhere except in "a proper Necessary" would receive five lashes. The prevalence of illness led to the establishment of many temporary hospitals as well the first American military hospital, founded in Yellow Springs, about ten miles west of Valley Forge. The three-story wood building had been a popular health spa and, once converted, could treat up to 300 sick men.

Although the winter actually was relatively mild, about 2,000 soldiers lost their lives due to harsh conditions in those terrible months. The death toll at Valley Forge exceeds the combined number of soldiers lost in the two nearest battles in the American Revolution: Brandywine and Germantown.

By early March, the weather allowed Baron Friedrich Wilhelm Augustus von Steuben to begin training his raw troops in military discipline. Up until this time, Washington's army demonstrated few signs of professional behavior. Unit sizes varied, and officers made no regular roll calls. Gambling, fighting, and absence from camp were not unusual. Soldiers had not even been trained to march in ranks or to use bayonets.

Steuben, who had risen to the rank of captain in the Prussian army, met Benjamin Franklin in Paris and offered his services to the American forces. He did not speak English, but he did speak French, which allowed him to work effectively with officers such as Alexander Hamilton and Nathanael Greene. The three men prepared a training program that was instituted by Steuben with an initial model company of 100 men. The Prussian officer also developed a much-needed sanitation program for the camp, setting a health standard for the U.S. Army that lasted more than 150 years. Among his innovations was the requirement that kitchens and latrines be placed at opposite ends of the camp.

Today, reminders of that difficult winter are part of the 3,600-acre Valley Forge National Historic Park. Earthen fortifications, rows of cannons, and the soldiers' log huts suggest the desperate straits the Continental Army faced there. Washington's restored stone headquarters still stand, and the park features statues of Steuben and another Revolutionary hero, General "Mad Anthony" Wayne, as well as a monument to Patriots of African Descent. Washington Memorial Chapel, with its tall stained glass windows, honors the revered leader of those who died there..

Artillery Park. Most of the cannon brought to Valley Forge were amassed in Artillery Park. Here, under the command of Brig. Gen. Henry Knox, artillery was stored and repaired and gun crews were trained and drilled. In the event of an attack, the cannon could be dispatched from this central location to wherever they were needed.

Old Fort Mifflin

When 18,000 British soldiers occupied Philadelphia in the autumn of 1777, they suffered a dramatic shortage of supplies, including ammunition, clothing, and food. To meet those needs, Great Britain wanted to use the Delaware River as a supply route, and Patriot forces naturally wanted to blockade that route. Fort Mifflin, named after its American builder, General Thomas Mifflin, stood on Mud Island near the intersection of the Schuylkill and Delaware Rivers—a position crucial to the success of the Patriot blockade. George Washington expressed the critical importance of the fort: "If the river defenses can be maintained, [British] General Howe's situation will not be the most agreeable; for if his supplies can be stopped by water, it may easily be done by land. . . . The acquisition of Philadelphia may, instead of his good fortune, prove his ruin."

Patriot troops stationed at Fort Mifflin tried to block ships from progressing up the Delaware by using chevaux-de-frise, or "iron horses," in the river channel. These weapons, consisting of five-foot-long sharpened spikes driven through large pieces of wood, were intended to hamper enemy vessels and force them into the fort's line of fire. Some British ships managed to slip past the iron horses, and in late October, the British began a sustained bombardment of the fort, which was isolated from American assistance. The British placed five artillery batteries on Province Island, and they were able to position a floating battery close to the fort. In November, the British fleet joined the attack. At times, 1,000 cannon shots occurred within a single hour. A Hessian mercenary fighting alongside the British described the ferocity of the attack: "The warships *Somerset*, *Experiment* and *Vigilant* sailed farther up the river very early this morning, and they fired at Mud Island and Fort Mifflin, which are strongly occupied by the enemy. The cannonade from these three ships lashed continuously for three days and nights, and in this time, there must have been more than twelve thousand shots fired on

*Old Fort Mifflin
Arsenal.*

both sides." This assault lasted almost two months and was the heaviest naval bombardment of the war.

Meanwhile, conditions within the fort were dreadful. Joseph Plumb Martin, who was stationed there, wrote, "It was utterly impossible to lie down to get any rest or sleep on account of the mud, if the enemy's shot would have suffered us to do so. Sometime some of the men, when overcome by fatigue and want of sleep, would slip away into the barracks to catch a nap of sleep, but it seldom happened that they all came out again alive. I was in this place a fortnight [two weeks] and can say in sincerity that I never lay down to sleep a minute in all that time."

American troops sought to repair battle damage on a daily basis, but eventually the fort's condition became dire, with only two guns remaining intact. As a result, Washington sent word to evacuate, and on November 15 the few hundred troops who had manned the fort went to Fort Mercer on the New Jersey side of the river. Fort Mercer, too, was abandoned a few days later: troops took with them

all of the supplies they could carry and set the fort on fire.

The Pennsylvania navy was also engaged in the Battle of Fort Mifflin, but the state's forty-two ships and boats were no match for the British navy. They were able to delay British attempts to claim the Delaware River, but in the end the state navy was damaged beyond repair and its men scuttled their own ships. Later, rebel forces mined the Delaware River with kegs full of explosives.

In the war's aftermath, Fort Mifflin served as part of the United States' coastal defenses. During the Civil War, a garrison of Union troops was assigned there to block Confederate vessels from traveling up the Delaware. It also served as a military storage and prison facility, during which time at least one Union Army deserter was executed there.

Over time, the narrow channel separating Mud Island from the shore has filled with soil, and, as a result, Fort Mifflin no longer stands on an island. Today, the fort has been restored to nineteenth-century standards and is available for tours.

Brandywine Battlefield State Park

Brandywine Battlefield State Park marks the site of a key confrontation in the Revolutionary War between American troops under the command of George Washington and British forces led by General William Howe. In the autumn of 1777, Howe set out to capture the rebellious colonies' capital, Philadelphia. British forces landed in what is now Elkton, Maryland, and began their march toward Pennsylvania. The British would cross the Brandywine River at Chadds Ford, and Washington chose that as the ideal place to confront the enemy. On September 9, he placed troops along the Brandywine from Pyle's Ford in the south to Wistar's Ford in the north in order to force a battle there.

The British forces gathered at Kennett Square, six miles west of the Chadds Ford crossing. Howe chose to have part of his troops march from there, as if they planned to face Washington's forces at Chadds Ford. Meanwhile, most of the British soldiers would go north of Wistar's Ford to cross at a ford unknown to Washington, then turn and attack American forces. On September 11, the day planned for the attack, fog obscured the British troops'

The Marquis de Lafayette's headquarters, the house of Gideon Gilpin, a Quaker farmer.

movements. The trapped Americans were defeated and retreated to Chester when night came. Washington's forces, which had amounted to nearly 15,000 men, stood at only 6,000 after the battle. In the next few days, Washington continued to try—unsuccessfully—to block Howe's advance on Philadelphia.

Congress eventually fled to Lancaster and then to York, and important supplies, both military and otherwise, were moved out of Philadelphia to Reading. Howe then seized Philadelphia on September 26. British forces left Philadelphia the following May because of fears that the French, who were allied with the colonists, were planning an attack on New York. The Brandywine battle area has been designated a National Historic Landmark, and various events honor its history each year.

Top: Washington's headquarters in the farmhouse of Benjamin Ring, a Quaker farmer and miller.

Equestrian Statue of George Washington

An inspired representation of George Washington, long celebrated in Philadelphia as a conquering general and a grand leader, stands near the city's artistic center. Rudolph Siemering's 1897 equestrian statue of George Washington was placed at one of three fountains in Eakins Oval in front of the Philadelphia Museum of Art on the Benjamin Franklin Parkway in 1927. (The other two fountains honor Eli Kirk Price, a powerful force behind the creation of the parkway, and John Ericsson, who developed the *Monitor*, the ironclad ship used by the Union during the Civil War.)

Through his role in the two Continental Congresses, his leadership of the Revolutionary army and the Constitutional Convention, and his service in Philadelphia as the nation's first president, Washington earned a great level of affection from citizens of this city. When word reached Philadelphia in December 1799 that Washington had died, residents were shocked. Mayor Robert Wharton asked Christ Church to silence its bells for three days as a gesture of

mourning. Congress immediately adjourned, and black drapings darkened its chambers as well as local churches and Washington pew in Christ Church.

The city designated December 26 as a day of mourning. On this date, twelve days after Washington's death in Virginia, commemoration began with the firing of sixteen cannons. After that, a cannon sounded on each half hour until 11 a.m., at which time a procession of military companies and political leaders began at Sixth and Chestnut Streets. From there, they accompanied a symbolic bier to the Lutheran Church of Zion at Fourth and Cherry Streets, which offered more seating than any other church in the city. Anglican Bishop William White, longtime rector of Christ Church, led the service.

Siemering's statue represents just one of the area's many salutes to Washington since that day. Others include Washington Square, Washington Memorial Chapel at Valley Forge National Historic Park, and Washington Hall, a nineteenth-century concert hall.

Free Quaker Meeting House

William Penn, founder of the colony of Pennsylvania, was a Quaker who incorporated his religion's pacifistic and egalitarian beliefs into the very makeup of his colony. Not surprisingly, in its early days, Pennsylvania attracted many Quaker settlers who wanted to practice their religion without the fear of persecution they had faced in England. By 1750, Quakers made up just one-sixth of the colony's population, but they had become influential members of the community and were important proponents of Penn's peaceful ideals.

However, Philadelphia's Quakers found themselves divided on the issue of war when American colonists began to consider a revolution against English rule. Under great pressure from both within and without the church, a small group of Quakers decided to back the revolution and broke off from the rest of the denomination to form their own meetinghouse. In 1783, a home for this new group of Quakers, called "Free Quakers" or "Fighting Quakers," was built on Arch Street between Fifth and Sixth. The Georgian brick building designed by Sam Wetherill brought the number of Quaker meetinghouses in Philadelphia to five.

Between thirty and fifty Free Quakers took part in meetings, including members such as Betsy Ross, the legendary flagmaker; Thomas Mifflin, a general in the Continental Army and signer of the Constitution; and Clement Biddle, a colonel and quartermaster in the Continental Army. The Free Quakers eventually ceased to exist as a separate entity, with many members becoming Episcopalians. Around 1834, the meetinghouse was abandoned.

The building later functioned as a school, a plumbing warehouse, and a temporary home to the Apprentices' Library of Philadelphia, one of the earliest free circulating libraries in America. Work to restore the structure began in the 1960s, and at that time the building was moved thirty-three feet west to allow the widening of Fifth Street. The balcony seen today was added as part of this restoration work, but inside the meetinghouse are two original benches, and one of the original windows remains intact. The site's historical exhibits include a five-pointed star tissue pattern purportedly used by Betsy Ross to produce the first American flag.

Today, the Free Quaker Meeting House is part of Independence National Historic Park and serves as the headquarters for the Junior League of Philadelphia.

First Bank of the United States

Before the Constitution established a strong central government, the states functioned independently for the most part, minting their own currencies and managing international trade on their own. This extreme independence not only weakened the new nation's ability to compete for trade internationally, it made it extremely difficult to raise money to repay a national debt—such as the huge one incurred during the American Revolution.

When it became clear that this arrangement was unsatisfactory, the Constitutional Convention first created a centralized national government with George Washington at its head. Then, at the suggestion of Secretary of the Treasury Alexander Hamilton, the United States Congress approved a charter in 1791 that would create the Bank of the United States, and George Washington signed the measure into law. This bank, America's very first national financial institution, helped the young nation recover from its debt.

The bank was established in Philadelphia, then the nation's capital, where it was located in Carpenter's Hall from 1791 to 1795. It soon moved into its own newly built, $110,168 Neoclassical structure on Third Street between Chestnut and Walnut Streets, now the oldest bank building in the United States. The building's Classical facade was intended to recall the democracy of ancient Greece. An eagle, the young republic's national symbol, stands atop the two-story portico.

In 1811, Congress abolished the bank by allowing the twenty-year term of its charter to expire. Americans at that time were suspicious of banks in general, and uneasy with any institution that appeared to have the potential to claim a monopoly. Soon after the bank's closure, business leader Stephen Girard bought the building and used it for his own banking venture. The structure was refurbished in 1976 for the nation's bicentennial and is now part of Independence National Historic Park.

Second Bank of the United States

The Second Bank of the United States became the center of a long and nasty political fight, but there could be little debate that its building at 420 Chestnut Street is an excellent example of Greek Revival architecture. Built between 1819 and 1824, the bank was designed by William Strickland, who modeled it after the Parthenon.

The First Bank of the United States, founded to help alleviate the debt incurred during the Revolutionary War, had been allowed to die in 1811. But after the War of 1812 with Great Britain, the nation again faced a huge debt, and inflation was soaring because private banks were issuing notes while many Americans hoarded currency. Some thought the institution of a new national bank would again expedite financial recovery, and so Democratic-Republicans acted in 1816 to establish the Second Bank of the United States.

The bank succeeded in maintaining uniform currency and eased economic crises by controlling the amount of credit available. However, in the late 1820s, the bank's existence became a hot controversy after Democrat Andrew Jackson

became president. Jackson believed the bank's power presented a threat to the nation, and many farmers and Western pioneers agreed. Defending the institution were Nicholas Biddle, president of the bank, and more than 128,000 Americans who signed memorials to show their support. Only 17,027 signed similar memorials in opposition.

Strong in his convictions, Jackson vetoed a bill that would have renewed the bank's charter in 1832. He labeled the bank an unfair monopoly and argued that the Constitution did not give Congress the power to create such an institution. Officially, the bank ceased operation in 1836, when the charter expired. In fact, Jackson hastened its decline by withdrawing about $11 million in federal money, which he allocated to a number of state banks.

Today, the bank serves as a portrait gallery graced by images of Revolutionary heroes and early federal government leaders. Charles Willson Peale, the leading portrait painter of the Revolutionary era, produced many of the works now on display. Works by James Sharples and Thomas Sully also can be found in the collection.

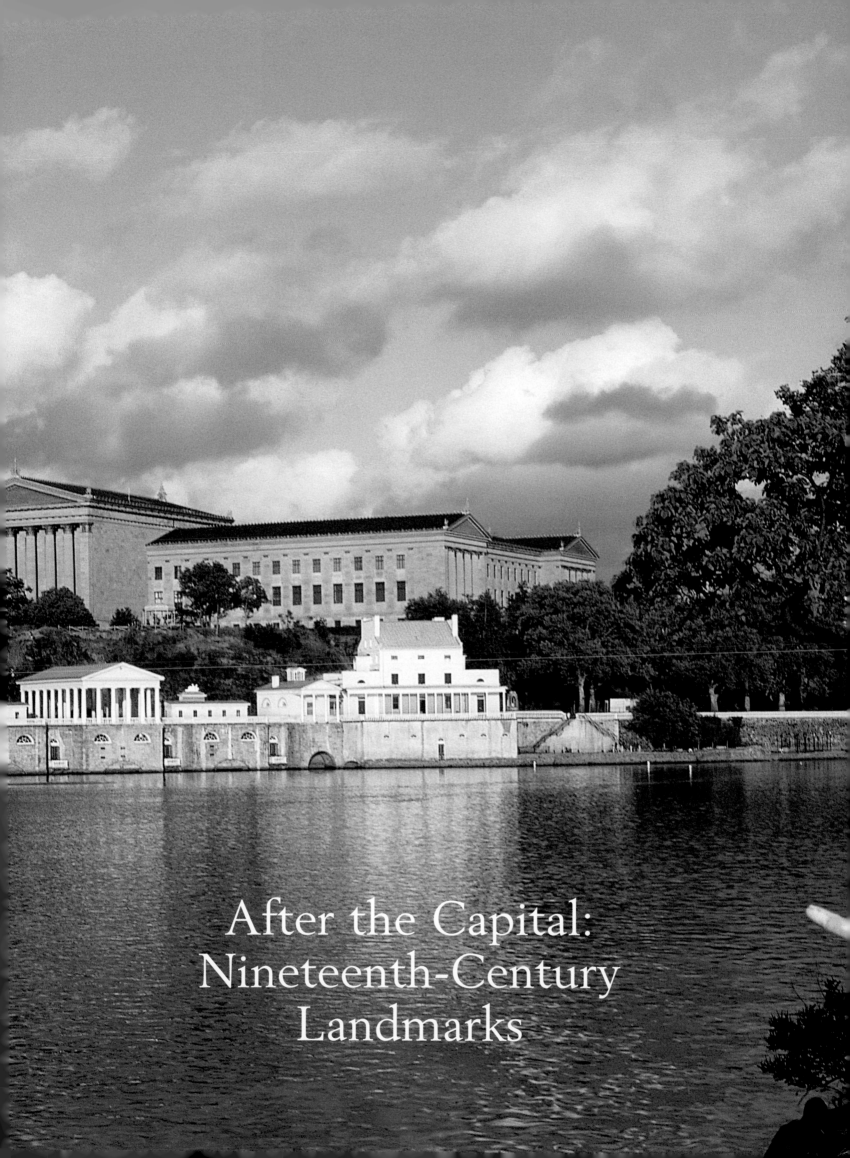

After the Capital:
Nineteenth-Century
Landmarks

Fairmount Waterworks

Built early in the nineteenth century to manage the delivery of water within the city, Philadelphia's Fairmount Waterworks became a model for other cities' water systems—and an unexpectedly popular tourist attraction. Dependency on easily contaminated wells and cisterns had contributed to yellow fever epidemics in the 1790s, so in 1799, several hundred citizens signed a petition demanding a new source of water.

The city's response began with the 1801 establishment of waterworks designed by engineer and architect Benjamin Henry Latrobe. Latrobe built a basin above Chestnut Street and a canal and tunnel that channeled the Schuylkill River water along Chestnut to Broad Street and down Broad Street to a pump house located in Centre Square, where City Hall now stands. At the pumping station, a steam engine raised the water thirty feet above ground level, creating a reservoir. From there, gravity guided the water through wooden pipes to homes and businesses all over the city.

Although Philadelphians flocked to see Latrobe's attractively designed pumping house, the overall project was a disaster. The waterworks were controversial from the start, because the Delaware and Schuylkill Canal Company opposed Latrobe's plan entirely, arguing that the city should draw water from Spring Mill Creek near Norristown. Then, the city hired Nicholas I.

Roosevelt to build steam engines to supply a million gallons of water per day. Roosevelt was a respected inventor—indeed, he would design the vertical paddle wheel that made Robert Fulton's steamboat possible a few years later—but his engines never lived up to projections. In the initial year of operation, when the waterworks served only a sugar refinery, four breweries, and sixty-three houses, it already became clear that Roosevelt's engines could not handle the flow of water necessary to serve the entire city. Not only that, but when Roosevelt claimed huge financial losses, the city had to provide partial financial restitution.

In the aftermath of this fiasco, Frederick Graff was hired as superintendent and engineer for the works in 1805. He remained a city employee for forty-two years and became the nation's most renowned expert on hydraulic engineering. More than thirty-five American cities, including New York and Boston, followed his advice, and designers of English water systems studied his designs on paper. Graff worked for five years to improve the system designed by Latrobe, but then decided that it would be more efficient to just build a new system with an intake farther upstream. His proposal moved the center of the works to Morris Hill, the current site of the Philadelphia Museum of Art, with a reservoir on top of the hill and a pumping station at the base. His plan received governmental approval in 1811, and Graff completed the project the following year. (Later, Morris Hill became popularly known as Fairmount, a name that originated in the seventeenth century with the city's designer, Thomas Holme, who described the hill as "Faire Mount.")

Graff's design introduced a number of never-before-seen innovations to the water system. He substituted cast-iron pipes for wooden logs and made it possible for a fire engine to hook up directly to fire hydrants. (Latrobe's design required that water be delivered from a ground-level pool by a hand pump into the tank of a fire engine.) He designed stopcocks, which blocked the flow of water if a pipe was broken or leaking. And he abandoned plans for powering the new system with a steam engine, opting instead for a hydraulic system that used waterwheels.

By 1822, Graff's ingenious creations were in place, and the waterworks had become a must-see phenomenon for travelers to the city. Not just awe at its mechanical wonders, but admiration for the natural and man-made beauty surrounding the Fairmount Waterworks led visitors to treat the site almost like a modern-day theme park. The waterworks were heralded for their attractive Greek Revival facades, constructed by the city in the final years of the project. Later, the site was made even more attractive by the addition of a monument to Graff, a fountain featuring William Rush's sculpture *Nymph of the Schuylkill*, and gardens and walkways around the buildings. One English visitor was stunned to witness the luxury enjoyed by the city's residents, who could be "immoderate water-drinkers." A prominent women's magazine, *Godey's Lady's Book*, even published a poem about the waterworks.

The waterworks made Philadelphia a leader in water system planning, but by the 1890s, they no longer served the entire city. For as long as it remained impossible to purify all city water, outbreaks of yellow fever and typhoid fever continued to plague the city. Thankfully, in 1909, a filtration system was installed that was able to accommodate all the city's water, and the outbreaks ceased. The waterworks functioned until 1911, when the facility became obsolete. The area then served as the city's aquarium for several decades, but today has been restored and is open to the public for tours.

Eastern State Penitentiary was one manifestation of a new correctional movement that asserted that inmates' behavior could be changed by "confinement in solitude with labor," and it became a model for other such prisons within the United States. It opened in Philadelphia in 1829, but construction of the original prison was not completed until 1836. The original complex covered eleven acres, had a state-of-the-art sewage system, and contained 450 cells with central heating. The building's cost—$780,000—made it one of the most expensive structures in the United States.

John Haviland, a British-born architect, gave the prison its unusual design: from the administration building at the center, cell blocks extend outward like the spokes of a wheel. The first three cell blocks built were one story high, but because of growing demand for prison space, blocks four through seven were built two stories high. Surrounding the prison is a stone wall that reaches twelve feet below ground and thirty feet above ground. A huge entrance and a tower jutting up from each corner of the wall make the whole complex reminiscent of a fortress.

Cell doors had slots for the delivery of food and an individual, outdoor exercise yard extended from every cell. This design eliminated the need to remove prisoners from their cells for meals and exercise, which might have brought them into unwanted contact with other prisoners. Under what became known as "the

Pennsylvania System," prisoners at Eastern State remained in solitary confinement throughout their imprisonment. They were prohibited from having any contact whatsoever with other prisoners, and masks were even manufactured to make it impossible for prisoners to communicate during the rare times when they had to be taken from their cells. Inmates who violated the prison's quietness by whistling or singing paid dearly for their violation by missing the main meal of the day for an entire week. The logic behind this approach was simple. Its advocates believed that, if left in solitude, prisoners would become sorry for their crimes.

Because both the design of the building and its correctional methods were unique, the prison actually attracted tourists. In 1858, more than 10,000 tourists visited the prison, the most visits in a single year while the prison was in operation. British novelist Charles Dickens visited the prison in 1842 and later wrote, "The System is rigid, strict and hopeless solitary confinement,

and I believe it, in its effects, to be cruel and wrong."

In 1913, the Pennsylvania System was abandoned and prisoners were allowed to interact, although group dining rooms did not open until 1924, one year after all female prisoners were transferred to a new prison in Muncie. (Most prisoners at Eastern State were male, but the first female inmate arrived just two years after the prison opened. Women at Eastern State were isolated in block two; in Muncie, a campus of small cottages awaited them.) In 1961, racial segregation ended in Eastern State's cell blocks.

Over a period of about 50 years, as the prison population in the United States exploded, seven new cell blocks were squeezed in between the existing ones. These had no room for exercise yards, and some of them even had three stories to hold more prisoners. By 1926, a penitentiary intended to house 250 inmates was home to 1,700. Many more additions were made, but the ever-growing demand for cells always eclipsed

Al Capone's cell.

the amount of space available. Finally, in 1970, most of the prison's inmates were moved to the State Correctional Institution at Graterford because of overcrowding and electrical and mechanical problems. After riots at the county prison in Holmesburg, county inmates were housed at the penitentiary in 1970 and 1971, but from that point on, Eastern State no longer housed prisoners.

The city purchased the prison from the state for about $400,000 in 1980. In 1994, the penitentiary opened for daily historic tours, and with funding from a private foundation, permanent museum exhibits were constructed the following year. Those exhibits testify to the unusual history of some of Eastern State Penitentiary's prisoners.

For example, a dog named Pep was sent there by Governor Gifford Pinchot in 1924. Some reports alleged that Pep killed a cat that belonged to the governor's wife, but others suggested that Pep was simply donated to the prison to improve morale. The prison's most famous inmate was Chicago gangster Al Capone, who was imprisoned there for eight months in 1929 and 1930. Other interesting exhibits tell of Eastern State's prison breaks, including the very first escape, in 1832, when the warden's waiter managed to lower himself from the roof of a building. The same man escaped the same way five years later. In 1923, Leo Callahan and five other prisoners escaped by scaling the east wall. Callahan is the only one of the prison's 142 escapees never to be recaptured.

Philadelphia Zoo

Philadelphia has the oldest zoo in the United States. Even before the Civil War, plans were under way to create a zoological garden adjacent to Fairmount Park. The first active step toward that end was taken when, in 1859, the state legislature incorporated the Zoological Society of Philadelphia. Among the society's early leaders was Joseph Leidy, a paleontologist and president of the Academy of Natural Sciences who also served in the Medical Department of the University of Pennsylvania. In the years following incorporation, stockholder subscriptions to the society financed construction of the zoo.

Architects Frank Furness and George W. Hewitt designed the entrance pavilions to the thirty-three-acre site at Thirty-Fourth Street and Girard Avenue. Furness also created plans for the Elephant House. Hewitt designed the Antelope House, which is still standing, although its original porches no longer exist.

When the zoo opened its gates in 1874, eager visitors arrived in horse-drawn carriages to gaze at creatures never before seen in the United States. At that time, the zoo featured forty-three species—with no camels, zebras, lions, or tigers among them. The first giraffes, lions, Bengal tiger,

Swan boat rides on Bird Lake.

and black leopard arrived later that year. Opening day was far from boring, though. Some members of the crowd were startled to see Jennie, an Indian elephant, apparently roaming about without restrictions. A few even fled in terror, not realizing that her chain was hidden by tall grass. The original cost of admission was twenty-five cents for adults and ten cents for children. During the year of the Centennial Exposition (1876), admission fees totaled $155,464—a figure unmatched in the seventy succeeding years.

Today, more than 1,600 exotic animals representing hundreds of species are on display in the forty-two-acre grounds, and more than a million visitors per year walk through the zoo's gates. Great efforts have been made to provide the animals with environments that are like their natural homes. All animals are treated at Philadelphia's Animal Health Center, one of the top animal hospitals in the United States, located in a secluded part of the zoo.

The Reptile and Amphibian House displays more than eighty species, and primates ranging from lemurs to gorillas are featured in the Primate Reserve. The first giant otters exhibited in the United States can be found in the zoo's Carnivore Kingdom. Philadelphia Zoo was also the first zoo in North America to provide a special zoo-within-a-zoo for youngsters. A

petting yard and live animal shows allow children to get closer to some of the animals. Visitors both young and old get daily opportunities to take part in feeding some of the animals.

Some animals that once had homes in the zoo are now extinct. Among them are the toolache wallaby, the passenger pigeon, the Carolina parakeet, and the West Indian monk seal. The twenty-first-century zoo includes a Rare Animal Conservation Center that places the spotlight on the zoo's many efforts to preserve endangered species. Among them are tree kangaroos, blue-eyed lemurs, naked mole rats, and giant Rodrigues fruit bats.

In addition to the fascinating animal life, the zoo's gardens display a broad array of plant life. Trees include the dogwood, poplar, flowering Japanese cherry, horse chestnut, yellowwood, codralla, Kentucky coffee tree, gingko, and sophora. Azalea, rhododendron, holly, and hydrangea are among the shrubbery plants within the grounds.

Also on the zoo grounds is Solitude, a mansion built in 1784 by William Penn's grandson John. Penn returned to England five years later and spent the rest of his life there. One of his descendants, however, stayed in the mansion in the early 1850s. Shortly afterward, the grounds—one of the last bits of Pennsylvania land owned by the Penn family—were sold and became part of Fairmount Park. Solitude features four unusual ceilings with special motifs, and one room contains John Penn's beautiful Sheraton bookcase. Much of the home is now used as office space, but zoo visitors are permitted to enter and tour it.

Cathedral Basilica of Saints Peter and Paul

The cathedral facing Logan Circle is a spiritual center for the Archdiocese of Philadelphia, which serves one of the nation's largest Catholic populations. It is also the oldest building on the Benjamin Franklin Parkway, with a foundation that was dedicated by church leaders in 1846, and construction of the building completed in 1864.

Designed by John Notman and Napoleon Le Brun, this sandstone, Roman-Corinthian-style showpiece's fortress-like structure may reflect a sense of insecurity in the city's Catholic community following anti-Catholic riots in 1844. Modeling the cathedral after the Lombard Church of St. Charles (San Carla al Corso) in Rome, Notman and Le Brun gave it a striking copper dome. The interior of the church is expansive and can seat up to 2,000 worshipers. Its ceiling, which soars to more than 156 feet, is adorned by half-ton chandeliers. In 1887, workers added a red marble canopy over the altar, behind which several of Philadelphia's past bishops and archbishops have been laid to rest.

Much of the church's planning and construction occurred during the tenure of the diocese's most famous leader, Saint John N. Neumann. Born in what is now the Czech Republic, Neumann came to the United States as a young man. During his lifetime, he was recognized for organizing the first diocesan parochial school system in the United States and for founding the nation's first Italian parish. He died just four years before the cathedral's completion. After his death, faithful Catholics began reporting that they had experienced miracles after praying to Bishop Neumann, claims that eventually won Neumann a declaration of sainthood from Pope John Paul II in 1977. The bishop remains one of few American Catholics ever to reach the level of sainthood.

In 1976, Paul John Paul II also declared the Philadelphia cathedral a basilica after it played a central role in the 41st International Eucharistic Congress, which brought together more than a million Catholics from around the world for an eight-day meeting in Philadelphia. Today, the cathedral basilica serves as both the diocese's home and the center of a lively urban parish of about 600 members. The congregation still celebrates mass every day of the year, making the stunning edifice not just a sparkling magnet to architecture buffs, but also a warm home-away-from-home for visiting Catholics.

Memorial Hall

In 1876, Philadelphia hosted an international Centennial Exhibition at Fairmount Park to mark the nation's 100th anniversary. To give the exhibition a totally new and impressive look, the Centennial Commission held an architectural competition. Four Philadelphia architectural firms won the right to build the four principal buildings: Main Building, Machinery Hall, Agricultural Hall, and Memorial Hall.

Memorial Hall, the only exhibition hall from the event that still stands, was the centerpiece of the festivities. From the beginning, planners intended that all the exhibition's more than 200 buildings would be temporary, except for Memorial Hall, which would serve as a permanent art museum after the exhibition's conclusion. Designed by the chief architect for the exhibition, 28-year-old engineer Herman J. Schwarzmann, the structure became America's first art museum built in the classic Beaux Arts tradition. The state and the city split the building's (then enormous) cost of over $1.5 million.

Since Memorial Hall was intended to become a home for priceless works of art, it was built entirely of granite, glass, and iron—all fireproof materials. Schwarzmann gave the building two impressive domes: a round inner one and a square outer one. On each of the building's four corners, an allegorical figure was used to signify industry, commerce, agriculture, and mining. The adornments on the building's terrace were later additions: The two huge bronze Pegasus statues, originally designed for the Vienna Opera House in 1863, were scheduled to be melted down when a Philadelphian bought them and gave them to the city. The bronze Spanish cannons were part of the fortifications that American troops captured in Cuba in 1896 during the Spanish-American War.

When the exhibition opened on May 10, bells all over the city tolled to mark the exciting occasion. According to the *New York Herald*, the big opening show attracted a crowd that was the "largest assembled on the North American continent"; official estimates set the crowd total at more than 186,000—including President Ulysses S. Grant and Emperor Dom Pedro of Brazil. By the exposition's closing in November, more than 8 million had attended.

Artwork on display at Memorial Hall during the exhibition included Philadelphia artist Thomas Eakins' *The Gross Clinic*, considered to be one of the finest nineteenth-century American works of art. The city also commissioned works in varying art forms for the opening-day festivities: poet John Greenleaf Whittier wrote "Centennial Hymn"; Sidney Lanier wrote "Meditation of Columbia"; and German composer Richard Wagner received $5,000 for his piece *Grand Centennial March*.

After the centennial, the Pennsylvania Museum and the School of Industrial Arts took possession of Memorial Hall. They reopened the building as an art museum and school one year later. The School of Industrial Arts later moved to another location, but the Pennsylvania Museum remained and was eventually renamed the Philadelphia Museum of Art. In 1928, the museum moved to its present home on the Benjamin Franklin Parkway, but it continued to house less important collections in Memorial Hall until the mid-1950s. In 1958, the Fairmount Park Commission, which now owns the building, began renovating the building to house offices and recreational facilities. Today, the historic hall is home to the Please Touch Museum, a fun and educational museum for children.

City Hall

Dominating the area that William Penn dubbed Centre Square is Philadelphia's City Hall, the largest municipal building in the United States—even bigger than the U.S. Capitol! After the entire county was consolidated with the city in 1854, plans to build a new city hall gained momentum. Old City Hall, which still stands on Independence Mall at the corner of Fifth and Chestnut Streets, simply was not big enough to handle the consolidated city's business. Six years after consolidation, the city held a design competition, which was won by John McArthur Jr.

Historical sources are not unanimous on the exact figure, but it is estimated that it took twenty to thirty years to erect the huge structure. Construction officially began in 1871 with excavations at the site, and the first foundation stone was laid the following year. Politics and business contributed to construction delays, but technological advances, such as the invention of electricity and elevators, also kept the building's plans in an almost constant state of revision. In 1879, studies began on methods of accommodating new technology for the building's water supply, heating, and ventilation. The first electrical lights were lit in 1881, and a hydraulic elevator was installed in 1886. City employees occupied individual sections as they were completed.

Throughout construction, disputes about payments also caused continued delays. In 1890, John McArthur died, and John Ord took over work as the main architect, but quit just three years later over a contract dispute. In January 1900, his replacement, W. Bleddyn Powell, told the Councils that almost $3 million in additional allocations were necessary to complete the building, but the Councils allocated only $625,517—just enough to keep the existing building in operation. The following year, Powell turned the building over to the city, but he did not consider it finished and remained a city employee until his death in 1910 because of continuing work on the structure.

The two features by which the building is best known are the William Penn statue that sits atop the tower and the tower clock. Alexander Milne Calder, working from space in the building's basement, completed the sculpture in November 1892. It was originally placed on display in the courtyard, but was moved to the top of the tower in 1894. The tower clock began its work at midnight on New Year's Day 1899, much to the delight of celebrating Philadelphians.

The east-west Market Street subway was constructed under the building between 1903 and 1908, but was relocated to a tunnel under the building between 1929 and 1934. The north-south Broad Street subway was constructed between 1915 and 1920, and the building's foundations were underpinned at the same time. In the late 1960s and early 1970s, Dilworth Plaza was added on the west side of the building.

Historians consider the story of City Hall a perfect example of the city's Iron Age, when graft-ridden and long-delayed construction of huge buildings was typical. The structure's design exemplifies the Second Empire Mode of French Renaissance Revival architecture, which had gone out of style by the time the building was completed. The Philadelphia essayist Agnes Repplier wrote of the building in 1898: "Its only claim to distinction should be the marvelous manner in which it combines bulk with sterling insignificance . . . squalid paltriness . . . decorations . . . mediocre or painfully grotesque."

Today, the building continues to run behind schedule as engineers work to bring it up-to-date with present-day building codes. Many city offices and courts have been moved into newer buildings nearby, but the building continues to function as City Hall.

Merchant's Exchange

For a long time, Philadelphia businessmen felt they could handle their transactions in very informal atmospheres. The city's earliest business was conducted in public venues such as the London Coffee House at the corner of Front and High (Market) Streets, where top merchants caught up on the day's news, negotiated agreements, held auctions, and debated political issues. Later on, much of this activity moved to the City Tavern on Second Street.

During the Jackson administration, however, the number of businessmen grew and the economy became more complicated, creating the need for a larger and more formal meeting place. In 1831, an elite group of the city's merchants joined forces to plan the construction of an official exchange. They chose William Strickland to design a building at Third and Walnut Streets, an oddly shaped lot due to its proximity to Dock Creek. Strickland gave the structure an unusual semicircular portico that took care of the awkward lot shape, and built space inside for a post office, several marine insurance companies, his own offices, and a coffee shop.

For more than thirty years, the building stood at the center of Philadelphia commerce as the place where businessmen traded stocks and goods and cut business deals. In 1866, as the center of financial activity was moving westward to Broad Street, the Merchant's Exchange was replaced by the Corn Exchange, which later gave way to the Philadelphia Stock Exchange. In 1952, Independence National Historic Park bought the old Merchant's Exchange building. Today, the National Park Service has some of its offices in the refurbished building, and visitors may enjoy exhibits about its architecture and history in the lobby.

Edgar Allan Poe House

Edgar Allan Poe lived in Philadelphia during some of his most productive years as a writer. Though perhaps best known for his poem "The Raven," Poe was a respected literary critic and short story writer in addition to being a poet. An undisputed innovator of American literature, he is generally cited as an early exemplar for the murder mystery writer and science fiction author.

Born in Boston in 1809, Poe was raised as a foster child of a tobacco exporter in Richmond. At 18 and without a college degree, he moved back to Boston, where he published his first book of poetry. He published a second volume of poems four years later. Poe apparently lived in Baltimore for a few years while writing stories for Baltimore and Philadelphia journals. He became editor of the *Southern Literary Messenger* in Richmond in 1835, and he subsequently

moved to New York, Philadelphia, back to New York, and then back to Richmond, where he died. His addiction to alcohol and reported use of illicit drugs may have contributed to his early death at the age of forty.

Poe and his family sojourned in Philadelphia from 1838 until 1844. While here, they rented several houses, but the only one that survives is the small brick house connected to 530 North Seventh Street that now carries his name. Poe lived there with his wife, Virginia; his mother-in-law, Maria Clemm; and their cat, Catterina. The family apparently moved to this house sometime between the autumn of 1842 and June 1843. While in the city, Poe wrote the short stories "The Gold Bug," "The Fall of the House of Usher," "The Tell-Tale Heart," and "The Murders in the Rue Morgue," as well as poems such as "The Haunted Palace" and "To Helen."

Masonic Temple

Philadelphia is recognized as the first city in the American colonies to host a Masonic Lodge. Early in the eighteenth century, few Masons had settled in the City of Brotherly Love, but those who had made their homes here began gathering in the 1720s. The first group founded St. John's Lodge, and by 1730, Benjamin Franklin's *Pennsylvania Gazette* reported that several Mason lodges operated within the colony of Pennsylvania.

In the eighteenth century, there were two Grand Lodges for Pennsylvania: the Moderns, who accepted new rituals designed by the Grand Lodge of England, and the Ancients, who clung to the old rituals. Most of the Moderns supported England in the American Revolution, and as a result, their organization disintegrated. The Grand Lodge of Pennsylvania "Ancients," founded in 1761, prevailed, and their 1873 temple remains the oldest grand lodge in the United States.

Today, the Masonic Temple is an architectural landmark in Philadelphia. The building on Broad Street has several rooms, each with a specific architectural theme, including Norman Hall, Oriental Hall, Ionic Hall, Gothic Hall, Egyptian Hall, Renaissance Hall, and Corinthian Hall. The temple is home to a library, founded in 1817, that now contains an impressive 75,000 volumes and 30,000 manuscript documents. Among its treasures is Benjamin Franklin's 1734 publication *The Constitutions of the Free-Masons*, the first Masonic book published in America. The temple also houses a museum, begun in 1908 and dedicated to department store–owner John Wanamaker. The museum holds many artifacts, including Franklin's Masonic sash and the Masonic apron awarded to George Washington by the Marquis de Lafayette in 1784.

B'nai B'rith, a Jewish service organization founded in New York City in 1843, commissioned a statue to honor "the people of the United States" for the nation's 1876 Centennial Exposition in Fairmount Park. Moses Jacob Ezekiel, the first internationally celebrated Jewish sculptor, was chosen to produce the statue. Born to a family of fourteen children in a poverty-stricken neighborhood of Richmond, Virginia, Ezekiel fought on the side of Confederate soldiers at the Battle of New Market during the Civil War. He began his artistic career in Europe after graduating from the Virginia Military Institution in 1866.

When he received the order for a statue recognizing religious liberty in the United States, Ezekiel carved the statue in his Rome studio and had it transported to Philadelphia. The dominant figure in the work is a woman wearing a cap bordered by thirteen stars representing the thirteen original colonies. In her left hand she holds the Constitution of the United States, and with her right arm she protects a youth, who represents the Genius of Faith. At the woman's feet, an eagle attacks a serpent that embodies religious intolerance. The sculptor's goal was to show that American democracy had defeated the evils of inequality and persecution.

More than a century after the centennial, the City of Philadelphia restored the statue and, in 1985, relocated it at the National Museum of American Jewish History at 55 N. Fifth Street on Independence Mall.

Laurel Hill Cemetery

butting Fairmount Park is Laurel Hill Cemetery, the first cemetery in the United States to be designed by an architect. It was founded by a leader of the Library Company of Philadelphia, John Jay Smith, who deliberately located the cemetery in a rural environment out of concern for the sanitation of crowded church burial grounds within the city. Smith acquired the land on the banks of the Schuylkill River in 1836, then asked architects to submit designs. He awarded the commission to John Notman, a young architect born in Scotland. Notman used the environment as his guide, creating a series of curving paths and natural amphitheaters from the slope along the river. His artistry was so successful that the scenic cemetery became a favorite picnicking spot for city dwellers in the nineteenth century.

The 100-acre cemetery became the final resting place for more than 70,000 people. When it became too crowded to accommodate more graves, West Laurel Hill Cemetery opened on the other side of the river. While most at the original Laurel Hill are buried simply, some lie in large, impressive mausoleums. Others there are distinguished by their activities in life: Thomas McKean, for example, who signed the Declaration of Independence, is among the dead, as is David Rittenhouse, for whom Rittenhouse Square is named. Many military commanders, particularly from the Civil War, were also buried there, including General George Meade, the Union leader who claimed victory at Gettysburg. In addition, three men who died when the *Titanic* sank in 1912 have markers in the cemetery. Their wives, all of whom survived the disaster at sea, are buried nearby. Other notables in the cemetery are Owen Wister, author of *The Virginian*, and Sarah Josepha Hale, editor of *Godey's Lady's Book* and author of "Mary Had a Little Lamb."

USS Olympia

The steel-hulled USS *Olympia* recalls many key moments in U.S. history, including many firsts and lasts. Commissioned in 1895, it is the oldest American warship of its type that is still afloat. It is also the last surviving product of a heavy investment the United States made in strengthening and updating its navy during the 1880s and '90s, a drive that gave a significant boost to steel shipbuilding in the country.

On the seas, the *Olympia* is best remembered as the flagship of Commodore George Dewey during the Battle of Manila Bay on May 1, 1898, in the Spanish-American War. U.S. naval forces crushed the Spanish navy in that battle, gaining control of the Philippines and making the United States a major force in world affairs for the first

time. The *Olympia* returned home from the war in 1899 and was decommissioned. In 1902, however, it was recommissioned, and over the next four years patrolled the Caribbean, the Atlantic, and the Mediterranean. The ship was again decommissioned in 1906, but it was used for U.S. Naval Academy training cruises in 1907, 1908, and 1909. In 1912, the ship was moved to Charleston, South Carolina, where it served as barracks for a reserve torpedo group. As World War I threatened U.S. shipping, it was recommissioned in 1916 as part of the Patrol Force Atlantic Fleet. After the United States entered the war, the ship patrolled Nova Scotia. In April 1918, it took part in Allied landings in Murmansk following the Russian Revolution. The ship's last major mission before its final decommission in 1922 was delivery of the Unknown Soldier of World War I for reburial at Arlington National Cemetery.

Thankfully, the *Olympia* survived the threat of being scrapped in 1954. Since 1996, visitors to Philadelphia have been able to admire the ship and learn about its history at the Independence Seaport Museum.

Victorian Boathouse Row

Visitors to Philadelphia are often charmed by the Victorian Boathouse Row north of the Fairmount Waterworks along the Schuylkill River's east bank. The Schuylkill Navy, the oldest amateur sporting association in the country, has ten member clubs, and those clubs began building permanent boathouses along the river in the 1850s. None of the original houses still stands, but some of the houses one sees today are almost as old, dating as far back as 1860.

Today, the fifteen houses reflect a broad array of architectural styles. The earlier houses were built in Gothic Revival or Italianate styles. Houses constructed in the 1870s and early 1880s exemplify the Victorian Gothic style common among Philadelphia buildings of the centennial era. The newest boathouse is Lloyd Hall, opened in 1998—the only boathouse built after 1904. The boathouses' owners are private clubs, who decorate the houses with twinkling lights year-round. The area around the houses is public land and is popular among rowers, joggers, and cyclists.

The Schuylkill Navy held its first regatta in coordination with the centennial celebration in 1876. Nowadays, exhibitions, races, and regattas are held yearly between May and July. The biggest event is Dad Vail, the largest college regatta in the United States. For more than sixty years, Dad Vail has attracted teams from more than 100 colleges and universities to the Schuylkill—not to mention tens of thousands of spectators. The city is also the proud home of the oldest and largest high school regatta in the nation, the Stotesbury Cup Regatta, begun in 1927.

Union League

Philadelphians founded the Union League in 1862 to support the policies of Abraham Lincoln's Union government during the Civil War. Among its accomplishments in those turbulent times were the recruitment of fifteen infantry, cavalry, and artillery regiments and the printing of more than two million pro-Union pamphlets. Since that time, the Union League has offered support for the American military in wartime. The nonsectarian, non-partisan club's motto is "Love of Country Leads."

Occupying an entire block of Center City, the Union League's impressive home is a French Renaissance-style League House completed in 1865. The eight-story building's brick and brownstone facade is complemented by twin

circular staircases leading to the entrance. Inside, the club boasts a 26,000-volume library, including archival material from the Civil War period, such as regimental records, manuscripts, and letters. Even the walls of the Union League are rich with history, as visitors will note from the organization's prestigious art collection and many historical artifacts. Among the many honored guests welcomed at the League House over its history have been U.S. presidents, foreign heads of state, business leaders, and entertainers.

The Philadelphia Union League's example has helped to shape Union Leagues across the country. At one time, hundreds of such leagues existed, but today only a few remain. The league's current membership stands at 3,000.

Right: Union League Library.

E Pluribus Unum:
Greater Philadelphia Today

Philadelphia Naval Shipyard

The Philadelphia Naval Shipyard was the first naval shipyard in the United States, established in 1799 when Congress allocated more than $500,000 to the project. Its first home was in Southwark, but as the city grew, the shipyard moved farther south to League Island.

For more than 100 years, the shipyard's job encompassed both construction of new ships and conversion of existing ships for new tasks. During World War II, when swift construction was crucial, the shipyard produced a battleship, an aircraft carrier, and two cruisers within seven months. Despite such impressive achievements, the navy began turning to private companies for the production of new ships in the 1960s. The last ship built at the Philadelphia Naval Shipyard, the USS *Blue Ridge*, was completed in 1970. After that, the shipyard concentrated exclusively on repairs and overhauls. It specialized in fossil-fueled surface ships and gradually developed expertise in high-pressure steam turbine engines, combat systems, and electronics.

The 1991 Defense Base Closure and Realignment Commission, which attempted to reduce federal spending by closing low-priority military bases, recommended that the Philadelphia Naval Shipyard be closed after one last job on the USS *Kennedy*. A 24-month, complex overhaul of the ship was completed in September 1995, and the shipyard officially ended operations a year later. At the time of its closing, the shipyard employed about 7,000 civilians and housed almost 400 temporary and permanent buildings on its 904-acre site.

Today, the shipyard is known as the Kvaerner Philadelphia Shipyard Inc., a private enterprise run by Europe's largest shipbuilder, based in Norway. Kvaerner took over operations at the shipyard after receiving promises of significant government funding for the project. The company's first ship manufactured at the Philadelphia shipyard was completed in 2003.

Previous page: Philadelphia skyline across the Delaware River.

Benjamin Franklin Bridge

At almost two miles long, Benjamin Franklin Bridge was the longest suspension bridge in the world when it opened in 1926. The idea to build it arose early in the twentieth century, but talk of a bridge between Philadelphia and Camden had been going on since 1818. At that time, bridge technology made it difficult to design a bridge that could be both long enough to span the entire Delaware and high enough to allow ship traffic. It was not until 1913, when more and more city residents started driving cars and bridge technology had become more advanced, that the talk became serious.

Five years later, Pennsylvania and New Jersey began studying the area and planning for the bridge. Eventually, decision-makers decided upon a suspension bridge from Vine and Race Streets in Philadelphia to Linden Street in Camden. (In a suspension bridge, the roadway hangs from cables anchored at either end of the bridge and is supported in the middle by intermediate towers built into the riverbed.) In 1922, architect Paul

Cret began construction based upon a plan by Rudolphe Modjeski, the bridge's chief engineer.

In 1925, with the Delaware River Bridge almost ready to open, a controversy erupted between Pennsylvania and New Jersey about charging tolls. Pennsylvania wanted passage on the bridge to be free; New Jersey favored toll booths. Pennsylvania eventually relented, and the bridge opened July 1, 1926, with toll booths on both sides. Almost immediately, it attracted a daily average of 35,000 vehicles, each paying a toll of twenty-five cents. When it opened, the bridge accommodated six lanes of motor vehicle traffic and two streetcar tracks, but the streetcar tracks were soon replaced by two more lanes for automobile traffic.

In 1956, the bridge was renamed the Benjamin Franklin Bridge. In 1992, one-way toll collection began. Drivers now pay tolls only in the westbound lanes; the eastbound lanes are free, allowing drivers to pass through without stopping.

Benjamin Franklin Parkway

Cutting a diagonal swath through Philadelphia's neat rectangular grid of north-south and east-west streets, Benjamin Franklin Parkway angles toward the northwest to connect Center City and Fairmount Park. The road has been compared to Paris's Champs-Elysées—which makes sense when one considers that the parkway's designers included Parisian architects Paul Cret and Jacques Gréber. As the scenic path to the Philadelphia Museum of Art, the Rodin Museum, and other cultural institutions, the parkway displays a wonderful mix of striking architecture and natural beauty.

The original vision for the thoroughfare came from Eli Kirk Price II, a member of the Fairmount Park Commission. Work on the street began in 1917, and just two years later the parkway was already a recognizable street. At that time, the Basilica-Cathedral of Saints Peter and Paul was already a well-established landmark, but many of the street's other well-known structures were not yet in place even when it opened in 1925. Ten years later, however, the Philadelphia Museum of Art was at the head of the avenue, and the Free Library of Philadelphia, the Franklin Institute, and the Rodin Museum (also designed by Cret and Gréber) were all in place as well.

In addition to its cultural institutions, the parkway is bordered by a series of international flags that hang above the street, making it the perfect route for parades. Its many fountains, small parks, and statues speak volumes about Philadelphia's heritage and about the wonderful possibilities for grassy splendor in an urban atmosphere.

Thirtieth Street Station

This eight-story, concrete-frame building is not only airy and elegant, it is the nation's largest train station and its second busiest. In 1925, the Pennsylvania Railroad and the city reached an agreement for a joint construction project. In exchange for new tunnel rights beneath the city, the railroad would surrender some land for city development. More important, the railroad and the city would join forces to build a new railroad station: Thirtieth Street Station, west of the Schuylkill River on Market Street between 29th and 30th Streets. Together with another, smaller station, Thirtieth Street Station replaced the old station near City Hall, which was seen as a deterrent to downtown development and had no space for expansion.

Because the start of construction of the station coincided with the onset of the Great Depression, the intended partnership between the government and the railroad had to be altered. In the end, the Public Works Administration had to finance completion of the project, but it was finished nevertheless in 1934.

At its opening, Thirtieth Street Station's transportation technology made it seem almost futuristic. Not only did it reflect the railroad's faith in electricity as *the* future power source for trains, but the concrete roof of the building was reinforced to allow for the landing of small aircraft. Over time, the station has undergone many changes. When it opened, it contained many unusual services for a train station, including a mortuary, a chapel, and a hospital space, all of which were subsequently converted for other uses.

In the 1960s, work was completed that made the station the grand terminus to what is now called John F. Kennedy Boulevard. Today, Thirtieth Street Station still serves both commuter and long-distance trains, as it always has, but it is also now home to Amtrak offices and retail shops.

Beth Sholom Synagogue

The Beth Sholom congregation was founded in 1919 in the Logan neighborhood of Philadelphia, where members constructed their first synagogue and school. In the 1950s, Beth Sholom was the city's first synagogue to migrate to the suburbs. There, north of Philadelphia in Elkins Park, the congregation dedicated in 1959 the only synagogue ever designed by the famed architect Frank Lloyd Wright.

Concrete walls anchored to the ground encompass the foundation buttresses for the three steel tripod girders that support the synagogue's sharply slanting walls, a design that makes it possible for the top floor to be free of internal supports. The main sanctuary seats more than 1,000; the Sisterhood Sanctuary on the lower floor is more intimate, with 242 seats. In the sanctuary's walls, translucent layers of wire glass and plastic are separated by air space that serves as insulation. In the daytime, natural light filters through the translucent walls, brightening the synagogue's interior; when nighttime falls, the whole structure glows because the artificial interior lighting flows outward.

Wright called the building a "luminous Mount Sinai," and some critics believe it is his most expressive house of worship. The architect's goal was to tie structural and decorative elements to Jewish ceremony, and indeed, observers have said that the sanctuary in particular reflects his "unmatched capacity to translate ritual into space and experience."

When the Museum of the Diaspora at Tel Aviv University chose two American synagogues to represent the Diaspora in the United States, it chose Beth Sholom and the Touro Synagogue in Newport, Rhode Island, the oldest synagogue in the United States. The museum explained its choice by describing Beth Sholom as exemplifying the modern synagogue. Today, the synagogue's congregation of more than 1,300 families remains open and active, concentrating much of its energy on helping newly immigrated Russian-Jewish families.

The two glass skyscrapers of Liberty Place are among the worst recognizable landmarks in the Philadelphia skyline.

Liberty Place

Until 1987, City Hall was Philadelphia's tallest building, and city architects honored an unwritten rule that no new building should exceed the height of William Penn's head on the statue that crowns it. That changed when Willard G. Rouse got permission for the two-tower Liberty Place project, in which both towers are taller than City Hall.

One Liberty Place is the grander of the pair, and it was constructed first, in 1987. It is Pennsylvania's tallest building and ranks among the twenty-five tallest buildings in the nation. Murray & Jahn Associates designed the post-modern, sixty-one-story tower to be reminiscent of the Chrysler Building in New York. Like that national landmark, One Liberty Place features a pyramidal top with a series of chevron setbacks

and sheathing of sparkling blue glass. Philadelphia's tallest is also outstanding for its state-of-the-art equipment. Its exterior includes a system to melt ice and snow, and it contains a special chilled-water plant that uses cooling towers, pumps, and chillers.

Two Liberty Place, completed in 1990, sports a similar but more modest design and has only fifty-eight stories. Together, One and Two Liberty Place take up a full city block bounded by Sixteenth, Seventeenth, Market, and Chestnut Streets. Both buildings house mostly office space, but One Liberty Place also includes a multistory hotel. Above an underground parking garage, the complex offers a public court, about seventy upscale retail shops, and a food court, making it a popular Center City locale.

Reading Terminal Headhouse and Market

The Philadelphia and Reading Railroad Company built the Reading Railroad Terminal at Twelfth and Arch Streets in 1893. The eight-story terminal was home to the company's administrative offices, ticket office, and lobby in Philadelphia, in addition to serving as the end of the line for millions of people traveling to Philadelphia for work, shopping, or tourism. Today, one might say its purpose hasn't changed all that much. Now converted into a huge, historic lobby for the Philadelphia Convention Center, the old train shed known as the Headhouse still draws in the crowds for meetings, eating, and sight-seeing.

The Philadelphia and Reading Railroad was established in 1833 to transport coal from mines,

often in western Pennsylvania, to industrial areas in eastern Pennsylvania, New Jersey, and Delaware. By the 1870s, the railroad had become the largest company in the world. In fact, it became so large that, in 1924, the Supreme Court declared it a monopoly and forced it to break up into two smaller concerns. Separated from its coal and iron enterprise, the Philadelphia and Reading Railroad Company adopted the simpler Reading Company as its official name.

Because coal shipments were so important to the company, it suffered after World War II when the nation began to shift to other sources of fuel. The railroad finally ceased operations at the Reading Terminal in 1984. At this time the City of Philadelphia took the opportunity to preserve the historic structure, which had been called upon its original completion one of the "handsomest terminal passenger stations" in the country. Not only was it especially beautiful, but, at the time of its construction, the terminal's roof was the biggest single-spanned iron roof in the United States; today, it is the oldest such roof in the world.

With these unique characteristics in mind, the City of Philadelphia's Redevelopment Authority purchased the building in 1993. Three years later it began remodeling the station's interior, transforming it into a new entrance for the Pennsylvania Convention Center and seeking retail developers for the site. When it opened as the new Convention Center entrance in 1998, it was clear that the terminal building had not just been preserved: the city had made it come alive again. It had even done an exceptional job finding retailers. The same year as the remodeled building opened, the Philadelphia Marriott opened a lovely 1,200-room hotel connected to the terminal, and the wildly popular Hard Rock Café became the first major retailer to open its doors at the site.

Another feature of the terminal, its food market, still survives. When the railroad company built the terminal, it bought the two nearby open-air markets and moved them under the terminal's train shed to create the Reading Terminal Market. Today, the building has a more modern look, but it still draws more than 80,000 shoppers each week. As at most farmers' markets, they come to buy fresh produce, dairy products, bakery goods, and meat.

The market also houses more than forty small restaurants that offer everything from Philly cheesesteaks to Peking Duck. It has become a favorite lunchtime destination for people working in or visiting Center City, and city redevelopment efforts in recent years have only broadened its appeal. The additional foot traffic from the Convention Center has exposed more tourists to the Reading Terminal Market as well.

John F. Kennedy Plaza (also known as "LOVE Park")

John F. Kennedy Plaza, located on the Benjamin Franklin Parkway, is a favorite city landmark. The site is also known as LOVE Park thanks to Robert Indiana's twenty-foot-high sculpture that spells out "LOVE," installed in the park in 1978.

The design for the park emerged in the undergraduate architecture thesis of Edmund Bacon at Cornell University. After Bacon became a city planner, he presented his old college plan in 1957 to Mayor Richardson Dilworth, who approved the park as a terminus for the parkway. In 1962, the parkway's elderly French creator, Jacques Gréber, returned to the city and signed off on changes in his creation. Three years later, park construction was completed based on a final design by architect Vincent Kling. The city dedicated the park as John F. Kennedy Plaza in 1967. The Fairmount Park Commission installed the park's fountain two years later.

In the 1990s, the park became a popular destination for skateboarders, in part because of the circular steps around the fountain. As a result, the city banned the use of skateboards in the area in 1994. Because the ban was not entirely successful, the park was renovated in 2002 to make it less appealing to skateboarders. Planters were placed to obstruct some ledges that might be tempting to them; others were covered with grass or shrubbery.

These changes brought protests by the Coalition to Free LOVE Park. Edmund Bacon himself, who was then 92, joined a 2002 protest of the skateboarding ban at the park, and in June 2004, DC Shoes offered the city a $1 million gift to reopen the park to skateboarders. In spite of all their efforts, the park remains closed to skateboarders today.

South Street

In colonial Philadelphia, South Street (then called Cedar Street) represented the city's southern boundary. Even then, it was a bustling area. Many residents of the street sold products ranging from food to fabrics out of the first floors of their homes. In the twentieth century, South Street has been compared with New York's Greenwich Village.

Under the threat of being overrun by a highway project, the area around South Street became rundown in the 1960s. In turn, the low cost of housing there attracted hippies, artists, and craftspeople, many of whom both lived and worked there—just like their colonial ancestors. South Street's reputation as a creative mecca even went nationwide when a Philadelphia singing group, the Orlons, reached No. 3 on the *Billboard* charts with their 1963 song about the neighborhood:

Where do all the hippies meet?
South Street, South Street!

The real South Street renaissance began in the 1970s, though, when the plans for a crosstown expressway through the area were scrapped. After its reprieve, the street became revitalized, and it has remained a unique retail venue for all sorts of products—both fine and quirky—ever since.

Today, South Street features restaurants ranging from simple delis to elegant eateries. Outdoor cafés offer an opportunity to watch offbeat and mundane representatives of humanity stroll down the street. Galleries, tattoo parlors, offices, nightclubs, theaters, and a wide array of retail stores all operate side by side. Over the last twenty years, expensive condominiums and apartments also have popped up in the neighborhood.

Clothespin

Claes Oldenburg's *Clothespin*, the forty-five-foot-high steel sculpture across from City Hall, is one of Philadelphia's more offbeat pieces of art. It looks like a giant clothespin, but some viewers have interpreted it as two people embracing, while others have seen in it the number 76 (which, perhaps coincidentally, is the year that the sculpture was completed). The whimsical piece of art has drawn public scorn as well as amusement. Its unusual nature earned it the honor of serving as the backdrop for a scene in the film *Trading Places*, starring Jamie Lee Curtis and Dan Ackroyd.

Oldenburg is Swedish, but he studied at Yale University and at the Art Institute of Chicago. He settled in New York in 1956 and produced several works inspired by his surroundings in the city's Lower East Side. After 1976, he began collaborating with his wife, Coosje van Bruggen, who is Dutch by birth. Together, they have produced more than forty large-scale works, including the University of Pennsylvania's *Split Button* and other works on display in Chicago, Nevada, California, Missouri, and Germany.

Logan Circle

Northwest Square, since transformed into Logan Circle, was one of the green areas that William Penn designated in his original plans for the city. Like Washington Square, the plot of clear land once served as a burial ground, but the dead were later moved elsewhere. Because this square was remote from the population center of the city until the mid-nineteenth century, public executions also were carried out here, the last of which occurred in 1823.

In 1825, the city decided to rename the square for James Logan, Penn's longtime representative in the colony. In the 1840s, local regulations made it illegal for livestock or wagons to be in the square, which, as one can imagine, significantly changed the atmosphere there. Later, grading was done to make the ground level. In 1917, Jacques Gréber, a French landscape architect who was one of the designers of the Benjamin Franklin Parkway, transformed Logan Square into Logan Circle, like the Place de la Concorde in Paris.

The Swann Memorial Fountain, also known as the Fountain of Three Rivers, was placed on the circle in 1925 when the Benjamin Franklin Parkway officially opened. The fountain honors Dr. Wilson Cary Swann, founder of the Philadelphia Fountain Society. Alexander Stirling Calder and architect Wilson Eyre Jr. designed what they envisioned as both a symbolic representation of the Delaware, Schuylkill, and Wissahickon Rivers and an adaptation of the standard river god sculptural motif. Calder sculpted Native American figures to represent the three bodies of water, and small frogs and turtles spray water toward the fifty-foot geyser in the fountain's center: a playful feature that attracts children as well as fun-loving adults.

Frederic Remington Statue

One highlight of Fairmount Park is Frederic Remington's equestrian statue *The Cowboy*. Born in Canton, New York, Remington studied briefly at the Yale School of Art and the Art Students League in New York before heading for the American frontier, where he traveled extensively. He began his career by producing illustrations for periodicals such as *Harpers Weekly*, and by 1886 he had become recognized as an artist who specialized in Western themes. Theodore Roosevelt, another enthusiast of the Old West, asked Remington in 1888 to produce illustrations for his book *Ranch Life and the Hunting Trails*.

In the mid-1890s, Remington discovered his talent for sculpting and began making bronze sculptures. In their production, he became the first American to reintroduce "lost wax casting," a system of foundry production that was commonly used in ancient Rome. This system allowed him to easily make changes to his works at each casting.

Perhaps more than any other artist's, Remington's body of work captures the image of the mythic West. Fortunately, he was particularly prolific, creating more than 3,000 drawings and paintings as well as 22 sculptures, a novel, a Broadway play, and more than 100 articles and stories. He produced only one monument, however: Philadelphia's *Cowboy*, unveiled in 1908, one year before the legendary artist's death.

Temple University's Bell Tower Plaza.

Temple University

Temple University was founded by Russell H. Conwell in the late nineteenth century. After an impoverished childhood in the Massachusetts countryside and service in the Union Army during the Civil War, Conwell joined the Baptist ministry in 1879. He proved to be a stunning orator and, just one year later, took over the leadership of Grace Baptist Church in North Philadelphia. Within ten years, he transformed the once-quiet church into a huge Baptist temple that could seat about 3,000 worshipers.

Branching out, Conwell started a night school for workingmen in the church basement in 1884. That school expanded into Temple College, chartered in 1888, and the college turned into Temple University in 1907. Conwell turned over to the university his vast earnings from more

than 6,000 speaking engagements in which he delivered his renowned lecture "Acres of Diamonds." The uplifting speech tied spirituality to money-making and raised the hopes of many of his listeners. In 1923, Conwell received the $10,000 Philadelphia Award, given annually to the area's outstanding citizen.

Temple University is now among the forty largest universities in the United States. Since 1965, it has been part of the Pennsylvania Commonwealth System of Higher Education. It is a comprehensive research university encompassing seventeen schools and colleges with more than 34,000 students. The university is based in North Philadelphia, but it also has four regional campuses, international campuses in Tokyo and Rome, and educational programs offered in several other nations.

E. P. Samuel Memorial Sculpture Garden

The E. P. Samuel Memorial Sculpture Garden, located at Kelly Drive along the Schuylkill River south of the Girard Avenue Bridge, comprises three terraces and seventeen sculptures. The works were commissioned over a thirty-year period with funds from a trust set up for the Fairmount Park Art Association by Ellen Phillips Samuel upon her death in 1913.

Samuel requested that the money be used to commission sculptural monuments that were "emblematic of the history of America." When the money became available after the 1929 death of her husband, the association set up a planning committee to decide how it would be spent. During the 1930s and '40s, the committee organized three international exhibitions at the Philadelphia Museum of Art to select artists whose work would be

The Spirit of Enterprise *by Jacques Lipchitz, 1960.*

Spanning the Continent *by Robert Laurent, 1937.*

appropriate for the sculpture garden. These shows not only presented the work of hundreds of artists from around the world: they also generated more money for the Samuel Memorial. Some of the more well-known artists whose works were chosen for inclusion were Robert Laurent, J. Wallace Kelly, John B. Flannagan, Helene Sardeau, Heinz Warneke, and Jacques Lipchitz.

Dedication of the memorial in 1961 ended the committee's work. One addition has been made since then: *Stone Age in America*, an 1887 work by John J. Boyle, was added to the memorial after being removed from the park's Sweetbriar Mansion area in 1985.

Pine Breeze Villa

Pine Breeze Villa is an elegant, authentic Japanese house that was built at Fairmount Park in 1953. It is also known simply as Japanese House and as *Shofuso*, a transliteration of the Japanese characters that spell out Pine Breeze Villa.

Yoshimura Junzo of Nagoya, Japan designed the house as a model of a late sixteenth- or early seventeenth-century Japanese palatial home. Typical of such a home, the house's central feature is a library, which contains a built-in *tsuke-shoin* desk and staggered shelving.

The house also contains a traditional kitchen with wood and dirt floors, a wood-fired stove, and a traditional cabinet. Apart from these effects, the house holds little furniture. In such homes in Japan, even bedding would be stored in a closet.

The house is connected by a small wooden bridge to a lovely tea house complex consisting of a small preparation room and another compact room—a pleasantly intimate venue for ceremonial tea.

Because the house was intended to exist in harmony with the surrounding garden, Junzo mapped out its construction in natural materials. The house is a raised platform made of hinoki wood. Tatami mats cover its floors, and the roof is simply multiple layers of hinoki wood supported by pillars. Interestingly, the entire building contains absolutely no structural nails. Sano Tansai designed the garden with traditional Japanese plants, such as bamboo, pine, hinoki cypress, flowering plum, and azalea. A stone pagoda from Kyoto and a life-size statue of Jizo, a Buddhist deity, can be found hidden among the plantlife. A nearby pond is home to a Japanese species of fish called *koi*.

Longwood Gardens

The land in Kennett Square now occupied by Longwood Gardens once was home to the Lenni Lenape Indians, but, in 1700, William Penn sold it to the Peirce family, a clan of Quaker farmers. Almost 100 years later, in 1798, Samuel and Joshua Peirce started an arboretum on their land. By the middle of the nineteenth century, it was already recognized as one of the nation's finest collections of trees.

In 1906, industrialist Pierre du Pont, then 36, purchased the land so that he could preserve the trees. Du Pont's great-grandfather, Eleuthère Irénée du Pont, came to the United States from France in 1800 and started the DuPont chemical company, which made the family wealthy. Gardening had been as much a tradition in the family as chemicals, and, through travel, du Pont had been exposed to both a variety of plant life and the most modern technology available to make a garden flourish. He enlarged the Peirce house itself and built onto it a conservatory to allow winter gardening, and placed extensive fountains around the property. By the 1930s, du Pont had established much of what is today known as Longwood Gardens. The fountains that now add so much to the beauty of the site he added later.

In 1946, du Pont placed the gardens in the hands of a foundation, which hired the gardens' first director after du Pont's death in 1954. Since the foundation took over the site, its attention has been directed at making Longwood Gardens more appealing as a public venue. This work has included expansion of greenhouse facilities, addition of horticultural exhibits, and a plant-breeding program.

Today, Longwood Gardens is considered one of the world's finest horticultural display gardens. It fills 1,050 acres of land with gardens, woodlands, and meadows showcasing at least 11,000 different plant types. The garden space is divided between twenty outdoor gardens and twenty indoor gardens, located in heated greenhouses that are open every day. Longwood presents 800 horticultural and performing arts events annually, and even offers educational programs that include training for careers in horticulture.

Benjamin Franklin statue by John Boyle, 1899, College Green, in front of College Hall.

University of Pennsylvania

Benjamin Franklin first presented his proposal for providing higher education to young Pennsylvanians in 1749. His vision was capsulized in a pamphlet, *Proposals for the Education of Youth in Pensilvania*. The college Franklin imagined would differ from other American colonial colleges in one important way. Its focus would not be on providing education for the clergy. What he suggested was, in fact, the nation's first liberal arts curriculum.

The university opened its doors downtown in 1751. In the late nineteenth century, it left Center City and moved across the Schuylkill River to West Philadelphia, where it has a 269-acre campus. That campus includes buildings designed by renowned architects Louis Kahn, Frank Furness, Eero Saarinen, Robert Venturi, and Denise Scott Brown.

Since its opening, the Ivy League university's prestigious graduates and accomplishments have distinguished it around the world. Nine signers of the Declaration of Independence and eleven signers of the Constitution were educated there, and fifteen Penn scholars have won Nobel Prizes. Penn was home to the nation's first medical school and teaching hospital, and the world's first electronic, large-scale, general-purpose digital computer, ENIAC, was introduced there in 1946. The University of Pennsylvania

The Arch on Locust Walk, by architect Thomas Martin, 1928.

Museum of Archaeology and Anthropology is recognized as one of the finest institutions of its type in the United States. In the midst of it all, on the campus's tree-lined Locust Walk, is a statue of the man who began it all: Benjamin Franklin.

Rittenhouse Square

Rittenhouse Square was one of the five squares laid out in the city's original street grid, designed by Thomas Holme and approved by William Penn. It was called simply the southwest square until 1825, at which time it was given the name of David Rittenhouse.

David Rittenhouse, who lived from 1732 to 1796, was a scion of William Rittenhouse, builder of the American colonies' first paper mill in Germantown, Pennsylvania. David Rittenhouse was a man of many talents. Although self-taught, he became an astronomer, clockmaker, and inventor. His 1763–64 survey of the Maryland-Pennsylvania boundary resolved a dispute between the Penn family and Lord Baltimore, and it was accepted by Charles Mason and Jeremiah Dixon as part of their research to identify the Mason-Dixon Line. Rittenhouse became an astronomy professor at the University of Pennsylvania, and he observed the 1769 transit of Venus. During the Revolutionary era, he served as a lawmaker in the General Assembly and was a member of the Pennsylvania Constitutional Convention. He also was the first director of the U.S. Mint and president of the American Philosophical Society.

Early colonists used the area around Rittenhouse Square as a pasture. By the close of the eighteenth century, the neighborhood's heavy supply of natural clay had led to the formation of a number of brickyards around the square. In the last half of the nineteenth century, a building boom west of Broad Street transformed the area into one of the most prestigious neighborhoods in the city. In 1913, French architect Paul Cret designed the square's signature entrances and its central plaza.

Today, Rittenhouse Square is ringed by condominium and apartment buildings, as well as hotels and retail establishments. Most of the fine old buildings that once stood around the square have been demolished. One notable exception is the Church of the Holy Trinity, designed by John Notman and built from 1857 to 1859. The church had one of the city's most chic congregations in the late nineteenth century, and one of its rectors, the Reverend Phillips Brooks, wrote the words to the popular song "O Little Town of Bethlehem."

Chinatown Friendship Gate.

Chinatown

Philadelphia's Chinatown is a unique and compact area that thrives on the byproducts of Asian culture. Surrounded by traditional downtown neighborhoods, Chinatown stands out with Chinese street signs, dead pigs stacked on the sidewalks, ducks hung upside down in restaurant windows, and other such unusual sights.

Lee Fong's, the neighborhood's first Chinese laundry, opened in the 1860s, and a plaque at 913 Race Street marks its location as well as the location of the neighborhood's first restaurant, Mei-Hsian Lou, opened in 1870. Other such business ventures popped up here and there, but Chinatown's growth was actually pretty slow until the 1940s. This was due partially to the fact that Chinatown was a "bachelor society," that is, populated primarily by male immigrants. That image changed after World War II, when more and more new immigrants arrived with their families.

These days, Chinatown is booming, but restaurants continue to be the primary interest of Philadelphians and tourists who go there. In addition to Cantonese, Szechuan, Mandarin, and Hunan cuisine from China, diners can now find Vietnamese, Burmese, Thai, and Asian fusion food in the neighborhood. Several restaurants also cater strictly to vegetarians. There is much more to the modern Chinatown, though, including a fortune cookie factory, video stores that sell Chinese films, a Chinese Christian church, grocery stores, and gift shops.

In 1984, Chinese artisans completed the Chinatown Friendship Gate at Tenth and Arch Streets. It was the product of a joint project between Philadelphia and its Chinese sister city, Tianjn. The multicolored arch depicts fire-breathing dragons, which, in Chinese legend, were believed to provide protection to the ancient Mandarins.

Morris Arboretum of the University of Pennsylvania.

Chestnut Hill

Chestnut Hill is one of the few neighborhoods in Philadelphia that offer both architectural and natural wonders. Nestled in the city's historic northwest section, its lovely and distinctive nineteenth- and twentieth-century homes stand between the breathtaking Wissahickon Gorge and Cresheim Valley.

Most prominent architects who have worked in Philadelphia over the last 150 years have made a contribution to Chestnut Hill. Included are Samuel Sloan's Victorian designs with an early Italianate flavor, G. W. and W. D. Hewitt's Queen Anne homes, Wilson Eyre's European-influenced work, Mellor Meigs and Howe's fine country houses, Horace Traumbauer's ornate Classical designs, and Louis I. Kahn's early modern works.

The neighborhood also contains the Morris Arboretum of the University of Pennsylvania, which doubles as both a public garden and an educational site. In 1887, siblings John and Lydia Morris built a summer home named Compton in Chestnut Hill. Around the home, they created a landscape that reflected their love of beauty and knowledge of plant life. To promote the study of horticulture and botany, they planned a school and laboratory at Compton, which became part of the Morris Arboretum of the University of Pennsylvania in 1932. The site is also the official arboretum of the Commonwealth of Pennsylvania, and so provides research and educational services to state agencies, civic organizations, and individuals.

Running along one side of Chestnut Hill is Wissahickon Park, dedicated in 1868—but a recreational venue since long before then. For most of the nineteenth century, Wissahickon Creek was a popular canoeing destination in the summer and ice-skating spot in the winter. Its flourishing forest and glistening waters inspired poets, such as John Kelpius, and artists, such as Richard William Greenleaf, Howard N. Watson, Thomas Linker, and Nicholas P. Santoleri. Today, it attracts crowds of joggers, mountain bikers, walkers, and hikers, as well as smaller numbers of fishermen, horseback riders, rock climbers, and skiers.

Rocky Balboa Statue

Sylvester Stallone popularized the character of boxer Rocky Balboa in the 1976 Academy Award-winning film *Rocky* and its sequels. From the very beginning of the film series, the character's strong connection to Philadelphia was apparent in scenes of him training on the city's streets, running through the Italian Market and up the steps at the Philadelphia Museum of Art.

In 1982, in a scene shot for *Rocky III*, a 1,500-pound, 9-foot-tall statue of Balboa was dedicated at the art museum. Created by Denver artist A. Thomas Schomberg, it depicts Rocky standing with clenched fists raised in the air. After the scene was shot, the moviemakers donated the statue to the museum, but it was rejected because museum leaders did not feel that it qual-

ified as art. Widespread public debate ensued about what should be done with the piece. Ultimately, the city placed it at the entrance of the Wachovia Spectrum, an arena at Eleventh and Pattison Streets. It briefly returned to the museum's steps in 1991 for the filming of *Rocky V*, but it went back to the Spectrum soon afterward. The statue has been featured in other films, including *Trading Places, Mannequin,* and *Philadelphia*.

Schomberg also designed two other statues for *Rocky III*. In 2003, the International Institute for Sport and Olympic History, a nonprofit educational, literary, and research organization, attempted to auction off one of them for $5 million . . . but failed.

Manayunk

The area around the rapids on the Schuylkill River above the Wissahickon Creek originally carried the name Flat Rock, but in 1824 residents met and decided to adopt a new town name. Manayunk sprang from the Lenni Lenape name for the area, *manaiung*, "where we go to drink."

The name is fitting—even today. Ever since the Schuylkill Navigation Company redirected the river's flow to complete the Manayunk Canal in 1819, water has been the secret to Manayunk's fortunes. The canal produced dual advantages for the area: First, it made river transportation easier, both to inland rural Pennsylvania and to the Port of Philadelphia. Second, it offered the potential of running machinery with water power. In 1820, the first of many textile and paper mills already had opened in Manayunk, and three years later, when the entire Schuylkill Canal System had been completed, Manayunk was well situated to become an industrial center.

The people who worked in the mills and lived in the cramped neighborhoods around them generally were immigrants. The first came from England, followed by Irish, Germans, Italians, and Poles. Through hard work and luck, some became mill owners themselves.

While the Civil War devastated the economies of many cities, Manayunk made the transition from cotton to wool textiles and persevered by producing blankets during the war. However, as other power sources were developed, water power no longer remained essential to factories, and that allowed businessmen to build plants wherever they wanted. After the beginning of the twentieth century, textile factories began leaving the Northeast—including Manayunk—to make the most of the cheaper labor force available in the South.

Today, Manayunk is a trendy Philadelphia neighborhood of sought-after homes and fashionable restaurants. It houses a mixture of upscale retail stores selling antiques, gourmet groceries, furniture, crafts, and stylish clothes.

Citizens Bank Park

Citizens Bank Park is the twenty-first century home of the Philadelphia Phillies, founded in 1883. It is a partial replacement for Veterans Stadium, which did double duty as a baseball and football field before the new park's construction. Its still-short history began in November 2000, when Mayor John Street announced that the city was going to replace "the Vet" with a new baseball field for the Phillies and a new football stadium for the Philadelphia Eagles. Street promised that "the sports complex will be unmatched in the country."

A few weeks after that promise was made, City Council made its fulfillment possible by approving a $1 billion stadium deal. The following year, the city purchased the land for the South Philadelphia complex, and the council approved lease agreements for both teams. Architectural plans for the new, 43,500-seat ballpark were unveiled, and excavation began in early 2002. As construction neared completion in late 2003, installation of a natural grass and dirt field began.

The Vet, long considered one of the worst baseball fields in the nation because of its Astroturf field, was demolished in 2004. The thirty-three-year-old stadium had hosted World Series games in 1980, 1983, and 1993, but the Phillies were victorious only in 1980. As 2004 progressed toward the new ballpark's official opening on April 12, a replica of the Liberty Bell was fashioned, a ten-foot statue of Phillies legend Mike Schmidt by artist Zenos Frudakis was bronzed, and an eleven-ton Citizens Bank Park sign was installed. Because of its natural turf and its exclusive dedication to baseball, the park was well received by Phillies fans at the first home opener in the new park—even though the Cincinnati Reds won by three runs.

The new ballpark pays homage not just to the history of the Phillies, but to the history of baseball in the city in general. There is a display about the old Negro Leagues in professional baseball, for example, and the Philadelphia A's are honored at the park by a statue of Connie Mack relocated from the Vet to the entrance of the

new field. Mack, a member of the Baseball Hall of Fame, was owner-manager of the A's and led the team to nine American League pennants. Originally, his statue stood near Shibe Park, otherwise known as Connie Mack Stadium, which was home to both the A's and the Phillies until it was demolished in 1976.

The Washington Nationals play against the Philadelphia Phillies at Citizens Bank Park in Philadelphia, Pennsylvania. The Phillies won the game 8–4. April 4, 2005.

Where Past, Present, and Future Meet: Cultural Treasures

The Fireman's Hall Museum, operated by the Philadelphia Fire Department, celebrates the history of firefighting in the City of Brotherly Love. It is located at 147 N. Second Street in an early twentieth-century firehouse that was active until 1952. At one time, the firehouse was headquarters to the famous Engine Company No. 8, which traces its roots to the Union Fire Company, the American colonies' first volunteer firefighting team.

The museum's exhibits trace the development of firefighting since that very first company. The Union Fire Company was founded in 1736 by twenty-five charter members—among them city and provincial officials as well as affluent merchants—who had been urged to undertake the endeavor by Benjamin Franklin himself. During the eighteenth century, Philadelphians placed leather buckets alongside their front doors. If an alarm was raised by shouting or bells, residents ran from their houses and formed a line, passing buckets of water from the nearest river to the site of the fire. In 1752, the city made an important acquisition when it purchased a large fire bell, and, by 1803, Schuylkill River water was kept in wooden trunks so that it would be available in case of fire. Philadelphia abandoned its dependence on volunteer fire departments in 1871, when it professionalized fire protection.

A brass pole, like those firefighters have used over the years to rush to their trucks, extends from the third floor of the museum to the first.

Previous page: Clenny Run, Winterthur.

Right: Metropolitan Steamer, built by the American LaFrance Company of Seneca Falls, New York, in 1907. Three horses pulled this apparatus for Philadelphia's Engine Company #11 until 1923.

Ten antique fire trucks, including early models drawn by hand or by horses, form the museum's centerpieces. A particularly eye-catching stained glass window depicts fire rescue efforts. Other highlights include a Spider Hose Reel made in 1804, a hand pumper built in 1815, a hand pumper reportedly used by Franklin himself, and a three-horse Metropolitan made in 1907. The museum also displays firefighting paraphernalia, such as helmets, axes, ladders, badges, posters, parade hats, hoses, and nozzles. Also not to be missed are early fire insurance policies and an interesting collection of fire marks: metal plates that were affixed to homes to indicate which insurance company had issued a policy protecting the house.

Franklin Institute Science Museum

The Franklin Institute was organized in 1824 to encourage scientific investigation, which played a large role in the busy life of Benjamin Franklin. Although he contributed to both the Declaration of Independence and the United States Constitution and worked as diplomat, printer, lawmaker, and civic leader, Franklin probably is still best known to American schoolchildren for his 1752 experiment to determine whether or not lightning was electricity. By flying a kite during a thunderstorm, he observed that electricity traveled into a key attached to the kite, thereby proving that lightning was indeed electricity.

In his own day, Franklin was also known for encouraging mechanically minded citizens to share information and to follow the spirit of exploration in science. Therefore, when some such Philadelphians chose to begin meeting thirty-four years after his death, they named their organization after Franklin. In the first meeting at the County Courthouse at Sixth and Chestnut Streets, the group adopted a constitution. That document declared the organization's goal to be "the promotion and encouragement of manufactures, and the mechanic and useful arts." The group's founders intended to present lectures by distinguished scientists and inventors, establish a library, evaluate new inventions, publish a journal, exhibit American-made products, and accumulate machines, minerals, and materials used in the mechanic arts.

Soon after its creation, the institute made its home at the current site of the Atwater Kent Museum, on the east side of Seventh Street between Market and Chestnut Streets. It remained there for a century until, in 1930, a fund-raising drive of just twelve days raised $5.1 million for a new science museum. The Franklin Institute Science Museum, at the corner of Twentieth Street and the Benjamin Franklin Parkway, opened its doors January 1, 1934.

Today, the museum is known for presentations of IMAX movies in its Omniverse Theater and for its hands-on learning opportunities. For example, museum-goers can walk through a model of a huge human heart—not an exercise recommended for the claustrophobic. In the Electricity Exhibit, visitors can enjoy a hair-raising experience in "Ben's Curiosity Shop" thanks to ol' Ben's static generator.

Aero Memorial World War I.

Heralding a long tradition, the Mummers Museum celebrates the often-gaudy, always-colorful performances of the Mummers, who march in Philadelphia's annual Mummers Parade. The term "Mummer" comes from the Old French *momer*, which refers to a masked celebrant. The parade's official beginning can be traced to 1901 in South Philadelphia. However, the tradition of the Mummers' holiday costumes and celebration dates back to the colonial era, and the seeds of those customs traveled across the Atlantic from Europe and Africa.

Each New Year's Day, the Mummers don costumes flowing with feathers and sparkling with sequins and strut down the street playing instruments like banjoes, horns, kazoos, and glockenspiels. Now, more than 10,000 people march each year, and the parade lasts all day. Mummers bands are highly competitive, as their performances are ranked by a panel of judges. The bands are divided between string bands, the fancy division, and the comics.

The museum was one of the smallest of a group of such institutions created as part of the 1976 bicentennial celebration. The Mummers' songs, design sketches used to create costumes, authentic uniforms, and memorabilia are preserved in the exhibits. Visitors can view filmed highlights of past parades, punch buttons to produce their own Mummers' medley, and even learn the Mummers' strut.

African-American Museum in Philadelphia

The African-American Museum in Philadelphia, located at Seventh and Arch Streets, was founded in 1976 as part of the national bicentennial celebration. Originally called the Afro-American Historical and Cultural Museum, the institution was the nation's first municipally financed body for the preservation, interpretation, and exhibition of African-American heritage.

The museum collects evidence and artifacts of the material and intellectual cultures of African-Americans in Philadelphia, the Delaware Valley, and the Commonwealth of Pennsylvania in particular, and throughout the Americas in general. The collection now includes more than 500,000 documents, images, and objects, including folk art, furnishings, costumes, memorabilia, photos, and books. Items are displayed in four galleries and an auditorium, where they are organized into an exhibition on one of the museum's dominant themes: the African Diaspora, the Philadelphia Story, and the Contemporary Narrative.

The museum's goal is to portray the big picture of African-American life in the West. Its scope is therefore broad, encompassing family life, the civil rights movement, arts and entertainment, sports, medicine, politics, law, religion, architecture, and technology. The museum also contributes to the development of local African-American culture by conducting public programs that complement its exhibitions. Offerings include workshops, demonstrations, film showings, dance performances, poetry readings, book signings, concerts, storytelling, seminars, and lectures.

Moravian Pottery and Tile Works

The Moravian Pottery and Tile Works in Doylestown serves as a "working history" museum where handmade tiles are still produced in the late nineteenth-century fashion. Born in 1856, Henry Chapman Mercer reached adulthood just as the Industrial Revolution reached its peak. Nevertheless, he maintained a deep admiration for the old-fashioned ways of producing goods, and became an advocate of the Arts and Crafts Movement in America, which promoted handicrafts over industry's machine-made products.

When he undertook this project, Mercer's goal was to bring new life to the craft of pottery-making in Bucks County. His initial efforts failed, and, as a result, he quickly diverted his attention to the production of tiles and mosaics, which could be used in ceilings, walls, and floors. Although he was an archaeologist by trade, Mercer had great artistic talent. He produced mosaics so remarkable that the state commissioned him to depict 377 scenes reflecting Pennsylvania's history and natural landscape for placement in the Capitol's red tile floors. His tiles can also be found in buildings across the United States and around the world.

Mercer oversaw the pottery works from 1898 until his death in 1930. Today, the facility continues to make replicas of his work using techniques similar to his own. To visitors, the works also offers tours and tile-making workshops; for more serious parties, apprenticeships in ceramics are available. The Tile Works building is interesting and attractive in its own right, reflecting the Spanish influence on Mission architecture—and, naturally, wonderfully decorated with a unique and diverse gallery of tiles.

Rodin Museum

Movie theater magnate Jules Mastbaum, a Philadelphia native, gave the Rodin Museum to his beloved hometown. Mastbaum began collecting Auguste Rodin's sculptures in 1923; by the time he died just three years later, he had the biggest collection of Rodin's works outside of Paris. To house those masterpieces, Mastbaum commissioned French Neoclassical architects Paul Cret and Jacques Gréber to design the museum building and its garden. Unfortunately, he did not live to see the opening of the museum in 1929, but he would no doubt have been very pleased.

The striking building houses 124 works, including bronze castings of many of Rodin's most famous works. Among them is *The Thinker*, perhaps the most renowned sculpture of all time. Other treasures include *The Burghers of Calais, Eternal Springtime*, and *Apotheosis to Victor Hugo*. Also in the museum is a bronze casting of *The Gates of Hell*, an ongoing work for Rodin from 1880 until his death thirty-seven years later. In addition to bronze sculptures, Mastbaum gathered drawings, prints, plaster studies, letters, and books related to Rodin, all of which now greatly enrich the museum. Since 1939, the institution has been under the administration of the Philadelphia Museum of Art.

Rodin was a French artist who lived from 1840 to 1917. He helped to redefine monumental public art, attempting to remain true to nature instead of following the traditional pattern of idealizing his subjects. His sculptures are praised for their outstanding expression of the inner sentiments of his subjects.

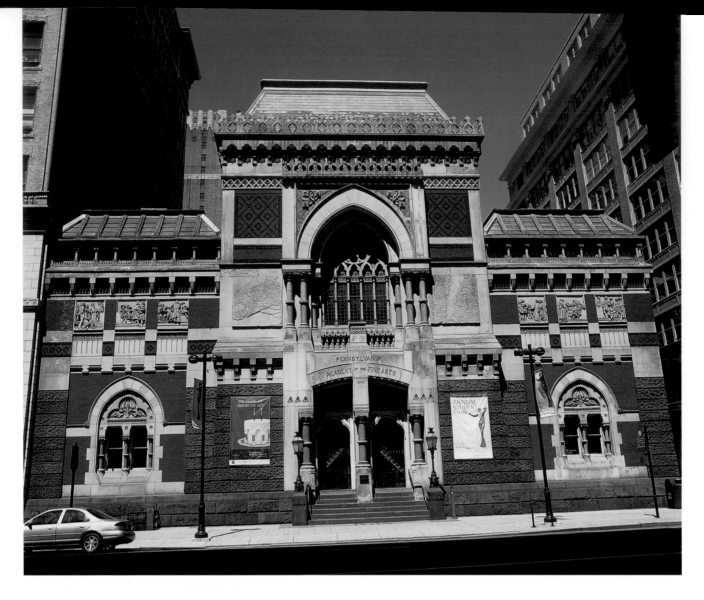

Pennsylvania Academy of the Fine Arts

The Pennsylvania Academy of the Fine Arts is the nation's oldest art school and museum. Philadelphia community leaders organized it in 1805 to accommodate a collection of art offered to the city by Joseph Allen Smith of South Carolina. Smith had put together the collection in Italy, including a wide variety of media from paintings and engravings to gems and cameos.

The academy's leaders built a small, Classical structure on the north side of Chestnut Street above Tenth Street. To augment Smith's gifts, they asked Nicholas Biddle, then working in Paris, to buy additional casts of Classical statues. He carried out that task with the advice of sculptor Jean Antoine Houdon, thus completing the academy's original collection.

In 1811, the academy began the nation's first art school and initiated an annual exhibition for artists. Originally, students were trained by working as apprentices, but by the mid-

nineteenth century, a group of local artists was teaching students in classes. The institution suffered a costly fire in 1845, but was able to reopen two years later. In 1876, the academy moved to its current home, a High Victorian Gothic-style building at Broad and Cherry Streets designed by Frank Furness. Artwork was displayed on the second floor of the building; the first floor was set up to accommodate classes. Because there was designated space set aside for instruction in the academy's new building, the school was able to broaden its acceptance policy at this time to permit any student who displayed talent to attend for free.

The academy has had some stars among its students in the past. Renowned artist and Philadelphia native Thomas Eakins was the towering figure there from 1876 until 1886, and he spent the remaining thirty years of his life working in Philadelphia. Mary Cassatt also

Right: View from the second floor of the Samuel M. V. Hamilton Building, looking down to the first-floor atrium.

studied at the academy, but she moved to Paris, where she became part of the Impressionist movement.

In the twentieth century, the academy sold much of its European collection to the Philadelphia Museum of Art. Today, it showcases primarily American art, featuring in particular the works of Philadelphia artist Charles Willson Peale, one of the museum's original founders, and those of Eakins. One of Gilbert Stuart's portraits of George Washington can be seen there, as can works by Benjamin West, Winslow Homer, John Singer Sargent, Edward Hopper, and Cecilia Beaux. The museum also offers special exhibits throughout the year, and the academy still trains aspiring artists.

Below: Washington Foyer, with Benjamin West's Death on the Pale Horse *in the background.*

Philadelphia Academy of Music

The Philadelphia Academy of Music is the nation's oldest grand opera house and one of the busiest performance halls in the world. Formerly home of the Philadelphia Orchestra, the academy is now used as a performance venue by the Opera Company of Philadelphia, the Pennsylvania Ballet, and the Philly Pops with Peter Nero.

Attempts to create an opera house for the city began as early as 1839, but the stock offering that financed the construction was not made until 1852. Two years later, organizers announced an architectural competition that was won by the Philadelphia firm of Napoleon Le Brun and Gustavus Runge. Construction began in 1855 and was completed two years later.

Most of the construction expense was directed toward making the inside of the building attractive. Because the building's initial supporters (wrongly) expected that the outside would be faced with marble at a later date, the exterior was left "perfectly plain and simple like a marketplace." Inside, the architects aimed to provide the best accoustics for an opera house while simultaneously giving all members of the audience a clear view of the stage with an "open horseshoe" design. The balconies are recessed upward in tiers, supported by fourteen Corinthian columns. Stylized medallions decorate the front of the first balcony. A huge chandelier with a circumference of fifty feet, a diameter of sixteen feet, and a weight of 5,000 pounds hangs in the concert hall. When installed, the chandelier produced light with 240 gas burners, but electric bulbs were installed in 1900.

The hall hosted the Republican National Convention in 1872, when President Ulysses S. Grant was nominated for a second term. Famous musical guests at the academy have included Enrico Caruso, Marian Anderson, Maria Callas, Aaron Copland, Gustav Mahler, Anna Pavlova, Luciano Pavarotti, Richard Strauss, Pyotor Illyich Tchaikovsky, and others.

Philadelphia Museum of Art

The Philadelphia Museum of Art is not just a stately terminus to the Benjamin Franklin Parkway: it is a treasury of artistic masterpieces from around the globe, on par with the greatest art museums in the world today. The roots of the museum were planted during the Centennial Exposition in 1876. Before the grand event, the state ordered construction of Memorial Hall in Fairmount Park to serve as an exhibition space for art, both for a temporary collection during the exposition and for the Philadelphia Museum of Art afterwards.

By the early twentieth century, it was obvious that the museum needed a larger home. In 1919, city-financed construction began on a new building for the institution at the site of the former reservoir for the Fairmount Waterworks. Horace Trumbauer and the firm Zantzinger, Borie, and Medary designed the stately edifice. The chief designer for Trumbauer was Julian Abele, one of the earliest African-American architects to gain prominence.

Within four years, the foundation was laid, and the wide steps to the building and the terracing of the granite hill were completed. To guarantee that the city would not abruptly end its financing of the project—something it did quite often in those days—the builders constructed the two outlying pavilions of the huge Neoclassical temple first, leaving the main portion to be constructed last. In 1924, temporary galleries were opened to accommodate three art collections that had been bequeathed to the museum in wills on the condition that the artwork be displayed within a reasonable time following the donors' deaths. The first permanent section of the museum to be completed, an exhibit of American and British art, opened its doors on March 26, 1928.

At its opening, the director of the museum was architectural historian Fiske Kimball. He was the man responsible for the museum's original organization, much of which survives today. He

Left: The Great Stair Hall. Poised at the top of the stairs is Augustus Saint-Gaudens' Diane, *which originally served as a weathervane for the old Madison Square Garden in New York.*

Opposite: Modern Contemporary Gallery 172. The sculpture (center) is Standing Woman *by Gaston Lachaise, 1912–1927. Visible on the left is de Kooning's* Noon *of 1947. On the right is first* Gyrations on 4 Planes, *an early Rothko work, and next to it is Pollock's* Male and Female.

decided that the first floor would house categorized collections, such as furniture, ceramics, and paintings. The second floor he reserved for a series of galleries that displayed masterpieces in historical sequence. He sent curators to England, Holland, China, Japan, and France to buy those masterpieces, while he went to work soliciting benefactors to pay for their purchases. In May 1929, the museum was able to report grand success: more than one million visitors had walked its halls during the previous year.

During the Great Depression, money for interior construction was difficult to find, but the museum did benefit from a Works Progress Administration grant for skilled laborers. And, even as the nation's economy collapsed, the museum's collections continued to grow. The heirs of Philadelphia artist Thomas Eakins made a large contribution of his paintings in 1929 and 1930. Another coup was the purchase of Edmond Foulc's collection of sculptures and furniture, including a marble and alabaster choir screen—a $1 million purchase that turned out to be the biggest single acquisition by a museum up until that date.

The period of the 1940s and 1950s, when many private collections were being dispersed to public galleries, was also a time of growth for the Philadelphia Museum of Art. The institution's Oriental Wing, which offers seven galleries displaying the arts of India, China, and Persia, opened in March 1940. In 1955, the Joseph Lees Williams Memorial Collection added a spectacular group of Oriental carpets to the museum's holdings. In 1958, fifteen galleries began to exhibit Philadelphia furniture and silver. One year later, the museum made a magnificent addition to its collections when it purchased thirteen Parisian tapestries designed by Peter Paul Rubens and Pietro da Cortona.

In the 1960s, continuing acquisitions bolstered the museum's reputation as the holder of many nineteenth- and twentieth-century masterpieces. This trend continued in the 1970s with the bicentennial "Gifts to Mark a Century" campaign. In 1977, the Armory was opened to showcase the collection of Otto Kretzschmar von Klienbusch, who had been the proud owner of the largest private twentieth-century collection of arms and armor. Other big purchases during these decades added a wealth of post-Impressionist paintings, Italian prints and drawings, and decorative Dutch tiles.

The museum's growth didn't slow down during the '80s, either. The Department of American Art was broadened by the 1983 combined purchase and gift of the Cadwalader Collection, which held five portraits by Charles Willson Peale as well as works by Gilbert Stuart and Thomas Sully. European galleries received the next expansion, in 1984, when the museum acquired 2,478 European old master drawings from the Pennsylvania Academy of Fine Arts. Just one year later, 43,000 more European old master and nineteenth-century prints from the academy were added.

In 1986, the trustees voted to begin a Landmark Renewal Fund drive to raise $50 million for renovation of the sixty-year-old museum building. Soon, the goal was raised to $60 million, all of which was raised by mid-1993. Suites of galleries were closed, renovated, and reopened in sequence, so that no more than one was ever unavailable to the public at any given time. The project was completed in September 1995.

Today, the Philadelphia Museum of Art is an elegant home for more than 300,000 works of art. Besides its permanent collection of great breadth, the museum offers special exhibitions and educational programs on a regular basis.

Kimmel Center for the Performing Arts

Opened in December 2001, the Kimmel Center for the Performing Arts was constructed to serve as home to the Philadelphia Orchestra. The building was named for Philadelphia philanthropist Sidney Kimmel and designed by architect Rafael Viñoly with the help of acoustician Russell Johnson of Artec Consultants Inc. The concert venue holds two performance spaces: the 2,500-seat Verizon Hall and the more intimate, 650-seat Perelman Theater, intended for chamber music concerts.

The Philadelphia Orchestra was founded in 1900. Only six music directors led the orchestra during its first century: Fritz Scheel (1900–1907), Carl Pohlig (1907–1912), Leopold Stokowski (1912–1941), Eugene Ormandy (1936–1980), Riccardo Muti (1980–1992), and Wolfgang Sawallisch (1993–2003). This relative infrequency of change has provided the orchestra with a particularly strong sense of continuity and cohesion. Christoph Eschenbach became the first new music conductor in the orchestra's second century when he picked up the baton in 2003.

Today, the Philadelphia Orchestra is recognized as one of the world's leading orchestras. It makes frequent international tours and offers an annual series of concerts at New York's Carnegie Hall. All in all, the orchestra presents more than 300 concerts and other musical performances each year, with all its home subscription concerts taking place at the Kimmel Center for the Performing Arts. Through its performances, recordings, broadcasts, and publications, the Philadelphia Orchestra has an impact on the lives of more than one million people a year.

Below: Verizon Hall.

Green Hills Farm

Green Hills Farm encompasses a complex of buildings that cover approximately fifty-eight acres in Bucks County. The farm is most famous as the former home of author Pearl S. Buck. Buck was born in West Virginia, but she spent most of the first forty years of her life in China, where her parents were Presbyterian missionaries. Turmoil in China and her own desire to be closer to her handicapped daughter and her would-be second husband, Richard Walsh, led her to move permanently to the United States in the mid-1930s. She purchased Green Hills Farm in 1933 and lived there until her death forty years later.

Buck's second novel, *The Good Earth*, detailed the life of a farmer in China. It was a bestseller in 1931 and 1932 and won the Pulitzer Prize in 1935. In all, Buck wrote more than seventy books, and, in 1938, received the Nobel Prize in literature.

The Green Hills farmhouse, built in 1835, reflects Buck's strength and durability. She made elaborate changes to the building when she bought it, the most significant of which was the addition of a two-story fieldstone wing. The property's oldest structure is a one-story summer kitchen, also built from stone. Historians estimate that the kitchen was constructed before the American Revolution.

The farmhouse now serves as a museum that is open to the public. It displays some of Buck's prestigious awards as well as Asian and early American objects. Buck, who adopted one child with her first husband and six with her second, founded what is now called Pearl S. Buck International. It is the result of a 1991 combination of two of Buck's humanitarian projects: one she initiated in 1949 to aid interracial adoption of Amerasian children and another that she began in 1964 to provide support to Amerasian children who are ineligible for adoption. The organization uses the house and outbuildings as its headquarters.

Mother and Child, *by Margaret A. Smith, 1990.*

Winterthur

Winterthur is an American country estate that was once owned by the prosperous du Pont family of Philadelphia. Jacques Antoine Bidermann, husband of Evelina du Pont, built the original twelve-room mansion in rural Delaware between 1837 and 1839. Bidermann chose to name the house Winterthur after his Swiss ancestral home. In 1867, after both of the Bidermanns had died, Evelina's brother Henry bought the house for his son, Henry Algernon du Pont.

Henry Algernon du Pont and his son, Henry Francis du Pont, chose to use the European country houses of the eighteenth and nineteenth centuries as models for expansion of Winterthur. Henry Algernon began the transformation in 1902 by constructing a new facade and a library wing. A year later, Henry Francis, who had recently graduated from Harvard University, took over managing the Winterthur household for his father. In 1909, he accepted responsibility for the extensive gardens and grounds as well. Henry Algernon died in 1927, and ownership of the house passed into his son's hands. Henry Francis added another new wing between 1928 and 1932, increasing the house's size by 100 percent.

Henry Francis also took the first step toward establishing the house as a museum: In 1930, he set up the Winterthur Corporation, a nonprofit, educational foundation that supports studies in American material culture and decorative arts. However, the museum did not open to the public until October 30, 1951. Since then, visitors to Winterthur have enjoyed its unequaled presentations of antiques and Americana. Winterthur's education program in Early American Culture was launched one year after the museum's opening. Today, Winterthur offers master's degrees in early American culture and in art conservation in conjunction with the University of Delaware. Since Henry Francis du Pont's death in 1969, additional galleries have opened at the museum to show visitors a glimpse of the period before the Industrial Revolution reshaped American life. Winterthur also maintains a sixty-acre garden that is open to the public, including a children's garden known as Enchanted Woods.

Memorial Day at the Mercer Museum.

Mercer Museum

Henry Chapman Mercer, a man of eclectic interests from Doylestown, Pennsylvania, started construction of the Mercer Museum in Bucks County in 1913. His motivation was to create a formal space for the exhibit of tools, which he believed told the story of human progress. With the help of eight day-laborers and a horse named Lucy, Mercer finished the six-story, reinforced-concrete building in June 1916.

After graduating from Harvard University, Mercer served as curator of American and Prehistoric Archaeology at the Museum of the University of Pennsylvania from 1894 to 1897. As an archaeologist, he conducted excavations in the Yucatan Peninsula and in the valleys of the Ohio, Delaware, and Tennessee Rivers. Privately, Mercer was an avid collector of items made

useless by the Industrial Revolution—that collection of artifacts provided the raw materials for his museum displays.

More than 60 percent of the museum's 50,000 inventoried artifacts are on display, and more than 80,000 visitors come to marvel at them each year. Items range from tiny clock-making implements to large modes of transportation, such as a Conestoga wagon, a whaling boat, carriages, and an antique fire engine. The exhibits encompass tools from more than sixty early American trades, including farming, printing, shoemaking, needleworking, woodworking, cider-making, and blacksmithing. The museum's oldest treasures are a whale oil lamp used by Native Americans more than 2,000 years ago and Native American tools dating from 6,000–8,000 BC.

National Constitution Center

The National Constitution Center places the spotlight on the U.S. Constitution, its history, and its impact on American life today. The architectural firm of Pei Cobb Freed & Partners designed the two-story, 160,000-square-foot National Constitution Center as the northernmost anchor of Independence Mall. The exhibit design firm of Ralph Appelbaum Associates created the innovative tools used to show visitors that, even today, the Constitution is a living document.

The National Constitution Center is an independent, nonpartisan, and nonprofit organization established by Congress in the Constitution Heritage Act of 1988, which President Ronald Reagan signed into law. Even before it had its own home, the center was hard at work raising awareness about the Constitution. For several years, the organization's main occupation was to present educational programs and honor outstanding Americans. It also conducted nationwide polls that measured Americans' understanding of the Constitution.

Then, on September 17, 2000—exactly 213 years after the U.S. Constitution was signed—the center entered a new era of its existence with the groundbreaking for its new building. President

Facade with Preamble.

Bill Clinton presided over the celebration, which included a naturalization ceremony for seventy-five new American citizens. The center opened almost three years later, on July 4, 2003, and welcomed about one million visitors in its first year of operation.

The center's main function is now to intrepret and teach about the unique document that established the framework for a federal government with checks and balances, a system that averts potential abuses of power. It details the history and the meaning of the Constitution for visitors through more than 100 multimedia and interactive exhibits, photographs, sculptures, films, texts, and artifacts. The center attracts buses full of schoolchildren, of course, but also interested adults. It frequently draws Philadelphians with presentations by outside speakers on contemporary issues related to the Constitution.

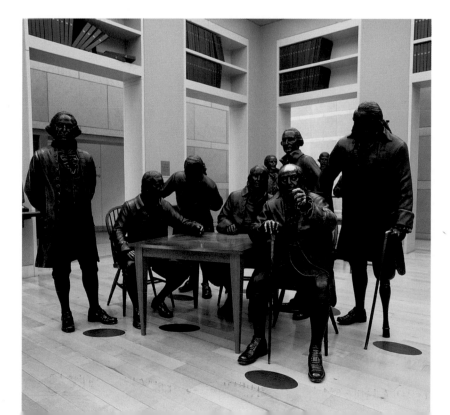

Signers' Hall.

Index